Socially Strong, Emotionally Secure

50 Activities to Promote
Resilience in Young Children

BY NEFERTITI BRUCE AND KAREN CAIRONE

with the Devereux Center for Resilient Children

Dedication

To Kevin, for helping me to learn the importance of teaching to the spirit of children

—NEFERTITI BRUCE

To Judy and Steve, my best role models for parenting and teaching

—KAREN CAIRONE

Acknowledgments

The authors wish to thank:

Linda Likins, for her leadership and vision, her passion for helping children, and her inspiration to all of us.

Paul LeBuffe and Martha Lindsay, for their insight and dedication, which were tremendously helpful in shaping this book.

Kate Kuhn, for her superb editing and guidance in bringing this book to life.

Rosanna Mollett, for her work on the cover, page design, and layout.

Wanda Newton from Devereux and Kathy Charner from Gryphon House, who were our 9th inning heroes.

About Devereux

Devereux is the nation's largest nonprofit educational and behavioral health care organization. In 1996, after nearly 75 years of providing behavioral health, rehabilitation, and special education services to individuals with special needs, Devereux expanded its mission into primary prevention. Responding to an emerging understanding of the preventable causes of some emotional and behavioral problems, Devereux created the Devereux Early Childhood Initiative. With a focus on promoting young children's healthy social and emotional development and resilience, to date the Devereux Early Childhood Initiative has reached more than three million children across the nation.

In 2009, the Devereux Center for Resilient Children (DCRC) was created to advance Devereux's commitment to primary prevention and promotion of resilience of all children. The DCRC encompasses the Devereux Early Childhood Initiative (DECI) as well as the emerging focus on school-age children.

Socially
STRONG
Emotionally
SECURE

50 Activities
to Promote
Resilience in
Young Children

Nefertiti Bruce and Karen Cairone

with the Devereux Center for Resilient Children

© 2011 The Devereux Foundation

For more information on The Devereux Foundation, visit our website at www.devereux.org.

Published by Gryphon House, Inc.
10770 Columbia Pike, Suite 201, Silver Spring, MD 20901
800.638.0928; 301.595.9500; 301.595.0051 (fax)
Visit us on the web at www.gryphonhouse.com

Library of Congress Cataloging-in-Publication Information

The Devereux Foundation.
 Socially strong, emotionally secure : 50 activities to promote resilience in young children / by Nefertiti Bruce and Karen Cairone, with The Devereux Foundation.
    p. cm.
 ISBN 978-0-87659-332-5
1. Social learning. 2. Resilience (Personality trait)--Study and teaching(Early childhood)--Activity programs. 3. Social skills--Study and teaching (Early childhood)--Activity programs. 4. Home and school. I. Cairone, Karen. II. Title.
 HQ783.B79 2010
 649'.7--dc22
                                              2010030861

Inspiring hope. Empowering lives.

Table of Contents

Introduction

Take a moment to think about how a mighty oak tree grows. A seed grows in rich soil and develops roots. Rain waters the seed and the sun shines on it. Over time, the tree grows strong and tall.

Now, consider how children grow, and in particular, how they develop socially and emotionally. When we plant healthy seeds and cultivate their roots properly, they grow up to be healthy socially and emotionally.

The famous poem from 1954 entitled, "Children Learn What They Live," by Dorothy Louise Law Nolte, ends by saying, "If a child lives with fairness, he learns justice. If a child lives with security he learns to have faith. If a child lives with acceptance and friendship, he learns to find love in the world." So, think about this... What are *you* helping your children learn?

Children can grow, discover, and learn best when they develop social and emotional skills early in life. Promoting optimal development of these skills, particularly in the early years, is important. The sooner we begin to make teaching these skills a priority, the better chance we have of helping children develop resilience.

Now more than ever, teaching must extend beyond the classroom. This resource book is designed to help in that effort. Each strategy and activity is designed for children ages three to eight, and offers a way to do the activity in both home and school environments. The goal is straightforward: To provide parents and teachers with simple activities that promote children's social and emotional development and resilience.

What Is Social Development?

Social development involves learning to form and value relationships with others. First friendships and the development of healthy social skills go hand-in-hand in the early years. Teachers and parents alike can promote these important social behaviors in young children by helping them establish and maintain friendships.

What Is Emotional Development?

Emotional development is closely related to social development and refers to how a child feels about himself or herself, about the people in his or her life, and about the environment in which he or she plays and lives. Both positive and negative emotions are important. Teachers and parents can help children understand, identify, and deal with their strong emotions and feelings.

What Is Resilience?

Resilience is the ability to recover from or adjust to misfortune or change, bounce back, and overcome the odds. Resilient children often possess qualities that help them get along well with others and "go with the flow."

Resilience is important for every child and adult, as we are all subject to the unknown; we cannot always anticipate when risk factors or stressful events will enter our lives. We think about resilience as having a "blanket in the back of your car." You never know when you will use it, but it is good to know that it is there if you are ever faced with a situation or occurrence where you need it.

How Can You Help Children Develop Resilience?

We believe every adult can help children build strong protective factors and strengthen resilience. Protective factors serve as buffers or supports that, when present, increase the well-being of children even when they are under stress.

Let's take a closer look at each of these important protective factors.

Attachment: The mutual, strong, long-lasting relationships between a child and significant adults such as parents, family members, and teachers. Children form strong attachments not only with their parents, but with other caring adults, including early childhood teachers and other adults with a consistent presence in their lives. The attachment bonds that children form in these early years often predict the quality of relationships they will have throughout life, as these early experiences become the model for future social interactions.

Initiative: The child's ability to use independent thought and action to meet his or her needs. As children develop healthy initiative, they learn to work and play attentively, independently, and cooperatively. Strong initiative in the early years prepares children to safely, actively, and eagerly explore their worlds, providing more learning experiences and opportunities for optimal growth and development.

Self-Control: The child's ability to experience a range of feelings and express them using the words and actions that society considers appropriate. This key protective factor helps children learn to control and regulate their own behavior and get along well with others. Children with healthy self-control in the preschool years typically have strong interpersonal qualities such as self-confidence and self-esteem.

We think about resilience as having a "blanket in the back of your car."

Learning to handle frustration and stress in the early years will help prepare children for challenges in the learning environment as well as in social settings.

Why Resilience Matters

It is up to adults to provide children with the skills necessary to navigate successfully through life. When the learning environment and home are safe, warm, and organized places with consistency in the care provided, children are set up for success. When children know where to go, what to do, and who will take care of them, they are free to focus on learning and having fun! Focusing on the factors related to resilience will not only significantly increase children's resilience, but also it will make them more socially and emotionally healthy, and they will be ready for today, tomorrow, and beyond.

Meaningful Activities Are Powerful Teaching Tools

The strategies and activities in this book promote social and emotional development and resilience in young children in both school and home settings. These meaningful experiences will help build children's strengths in their most important and influential settings and with the adults who are most invested in them.

The strategies and activities in this book are organized into five chapters:
- ▶ Supportive, Caring Practices
- ▶ Home and School Partnerships
- ▶ Activities and Experiences
- ▶ Daily Routines and Transitions
- ▶ Play and Learning Environment

Supportive, Caring Practices—The relationships between children and adults in a learning environment, and among the children themselves, are the basis for building a safe, strong, and caring community in which everyone is accepted, respected, and comfortable. The activities in the Supportive, Caring Practices chapter focus on helping children develop the skills needed for building and strengthening relationships. When supportive interactions are high quality and well planned, children's bonds with others will grow in this caring and safe setting. Children will feel confident and ready to explore.

Home and School Partnerships—When all the adults in a child's life become partners, with the shared goal of working together to meet the child's needs, they set a wonderful stage for success. In the Home and School Partnerships chapter, strategies and activities create opportunities for sharing resources between home and school and learning about and respecting cultural and individual differences.

Activities and Experiences—To promote the social development, emotional development, and resilience of young children, activities and experiences should encourage critical thinking skills, the use of imagination, and creative expression. The activities and ideas in the Activities and Experiences chapter promote all these, plus open-ended thinking, physical activity, and social and emotional learning.

Daily Routines and Transitions—What we do both during and in between everyday routines really affects how children grow and develop. Children develop trust and a sense of what to expect next when daily routines are predictable. In the Daily Routines chapter, strategies and activities help establish and maintain a consistent, yet flexible, structure and schedule for children—a huge contributor to developing a sense of belonging and community, cooperative participation, and engaged learning.

Playing and Learning Environment—Children do not need lots of expensive toys, furnishings, or other items that often hinder growth and development instead of promote it. What they do need are well-designed spaces, both at home and at school, that allow them to grow and learn. In the Playing and Learning Environment chapter, strategies focus on creating environments that are physically and emotionally geared to maximize learning and personal growth.

How to Use This Book

As you use the activities in this book, the goal is to enjoy the children's company while promoting their social development, emotional development, and resilience. You can start at the beginning, the middle, or even the end. We suggest that you spend time reading each of the activities included to help you decide where to begin. We have incuded reproducible at-home activity pages to hep reinforce skills that children learn in the classroom.

Remember, when doing ANY activity in your classroom or home, try viewing it through "social and emotional lenses" to see what skills you are building and supporting. When you consider the important areas of a young child's development, it is clear that the quality time you spend interacting with a child will promote resilience, initiative, attachment, and self-control in one way or another!

Certainly, no matter where you start, you and the child or children you nurture are in for a remarkable journey towards resilience. The result of this journey will be children who are happier, more cooperative, and, ultimately, more resilient.

Promoting Resilience Through Supportive, Caring Practices

Supportive interactions occur every day when teachers eagerly greet children as they arrive in the classroom, offering loving hugs and big hellos. Supportive interactions also occur when family members engage children in conversation about how it feels to be upset or scared about changes. Supportive interactions are the basis for relationship-building, and relationships are the foundation for the warm and caring bonds that help both children and adults feel safe. Young children experience their world as an environment of relationships, and these relationships affect just about every aspect of development—cognitive, social, emotional, and physical.

Carrying out supportive interaction strategies is not difficult, but it must become intentional. Intentional strategies are thought out and planned in advance, helping adults be more prepared for and mindful of their efforts to prevent challenging behaviors and promote healthy social and emotional development. When we are not intentional in our planning, our activities can seem forced, rushed, and lacking in meaning and purpose.

What Research Says

Relationships are the "active ingredients" in healthy human development. At their best, they promote competence and well-being, individualized responsiveness, mutual action-and-interaction, and an emotional connection to another human being, be it parent, peer, grandparent, aunt, uncle, neighbor, teacher, coach, or any other person who has an important impact on the child's early development.

In the words of the distinguished developmental psychologist Urie Bronfenbrenner, *"Somebody's got to be crazy about that kid. That's number one. First, last, and always."*

(National Scientific Council on the Developing Child, 2004: Young Children Develop in an Environment of Relationships).

A few simple ideas to keep in mind include:

▶ **Listen attentively**—Young children are full of laughter, stories, anecdotes, and simple tales of their lives. When a child shares with you, lean forward and make eye contact, asking questions such as, "Wow, this is interesting, can you tell me more?"

▶ **Display unwavering, genuine care and compassion**—In the classroom, let the children know you are happy to be their teacher. Call or send notes to children who may be ill, celebrate significant family events along with the family, and work with diligence to create a classroom community where every child and family feels respected and welcome. Casual conversations, celebration of birthdays, comments on a new haircut, or warm thoughts after recovering from a bad fall can set the example of care that children can learn from. Encourage families to let their child know that they are loved.

▶ **Say it with a smile**—Often, it is not what you say but how you say it. Practice saying, "I care" by giving the child a "thumbs up" from across the room or saying, "You're great just the way you are" by simply smiling at the child.

▶ **Mirror, mirror**—Help children find their strengths by mirroring back to them those things they do well, remembering to focus on both effort as well as end results. "Marcus, you have worked so hard on this puzzle, and now you have really got it!"

What's Ahead

In this chapter you will find everyday strategies that can be used to create strong supportive interactions and build three key social and emotional skills in children: initiative, attachment, and self-control.

When you use strategies that focus on supportive interactions, you support:

▶ Children's **initiative**. When children feel safe and cared for, this allows them to be risk takers, dreamers, and creative beings free to express themselves within safe limits set by those who love and care for them. In an environment rich in supportive interactions, children gain a love for learning.

▶ Children's **attachment**. Growth-promoting relationships are based on the continuous give-and-take between children and adults who can provide what nothing else in the world can offer–experiences that are individualized to each of the children's unique personality styles, are built on interests and capabilities, and that stimulate growth of the heart and the mind.

▶ Children's **self-control**. The warmth and support children receive influences the development of greater social competence, fewer behavior problems, and enhanced thinking and reasoning skills at school age.

10 Ways to Promote Resilience Using Supportive, Caring Practices

1. Help children learn the skills and behaviors used to play and learn with others.

2. Know what is developmentally appropriate for children, and maintain realistic expectations for each child as an individual.

3. Involve children in setting a few positively stated rules and guidelines.

4. Support children in building trusting relationships with caring adults.

5. Support children's growing independence and competence.

6. Help children understand their feelings and those of others.

7. Try to learn the reasons behind children's behavior, understanding that children will use challenging behavior as long as it continues to get them what they want or need.

8. Support cooperation, guiding children as they learn to take turns and work together.

9. Teach children problem-solving skills and encourage them to use their skills to resolve conflicts.

10. Create a safe, fun, and nurturing community of caring in which children can play, work, and learn.

Give Me a Hand

Helps children learn the skills and behaviors used to play and learn with others.

What Children Will Learn

This activity helps children start to recognize feelings in others and in themselves. This is the beginning of developing empathy. For children to fully understand the feelings of others, they need to be in tune with strong feelings in their own bodies. By helping give children some words to use in play situations, you are setting them up for more successful social and emotional interactions. Regularly talking about feelings and reviewing kind play words will help children on the journey to develop empathy, as well as helping them learn to become good friends to others.

Social and Emotional Skills Supported

Attachment, Initiative, Self-Control

Materials Needed

paintbrushes
washable tempera paint

What to Do

▶ Gather the children together and explain that you will be talking together about how it feels to work and play in friendly ways, and also how it feels when others don't play well together.

▶ Tell the children you are going to need their hands to help make this activity great!

▶ For each child, on the back of one hand, draw a happy face using the tempera paint and paintbrush. On the back of the other hand, draw a sad face.

▶ Remind the children to keep their hands away from their bodies and any items or materials nearby so that they don't get paint on themselves or anything else.

▶ Each time you describe a situation, ask the children to hold up the appropriate hand to show how they would feel. Here are some examples:

> *"How would you feel if your friend shared one of his cookies with you?"*

> *"How would you feel if your friend invited you to her birthday party?"*

NOTE: For a less "messy" variation, give the children two pieces of paper and invite them to create a happy face and a sad face using pens, markers, or crayons. Ask them to hold up the piece of paper with the face that matches the feeling.

Social & Emotional Lenses

Telling children to "use your words!" is often not enough; we need to help them learn the right words to use!

"How would you feel if your friend would not let you play with him?"

"How would you feel if you and your friends planted a garden together?"

"How would you feel if someone was teasing you?"

▶ Feel free to add other questions. Write down the children's ideas on paper. You might create a chart with a smiley face on top of one column and a sad face on top of the other column. As you review each situation, write a few words from the children in the appropriate column.

▶ End this activity by explaining to the children that they have words they can use to help them play and learn with others. Here are a few simple suggestions:

May I play with you?

When you are finished, may I have a turn?

Please stop it. I don't like it.

Can we take turns?

Do you want to play together?

Thank you for asking me to play. I want to finish this first.

I like this. Can we do it together?

Give Me a Hand

Try this activity at home to reinforce what your child learned about recognizing his feelings and the feelings of others.

What Your Child Will Learn

This activity will help your child or children start to recognize feelings in others and in themselves. This is the beginning of developing empathy. For children to fully understand the feelings of others, they need to be in tune with strong feelings in their own bodies. By helping give children some words to use in play situations, you are setting them up for more successful social and emotional interactions. Regularly talking about feelings and reviewing kind play words will help your child or children on the journey to develop empathy, as well as helping them learn to become good friends to others.

Materials Needed

paintbrushes, magazine or book pictures of sad and happy children, washable tempera paint

What to Do

▶ On the back of one of your child's hands, draw a happy face using the tempera paint and paintbrush. On the back of the other hand, draw a sad face.

▶ Help your child think of situations with friends that might make everyone feel happy or sad. Ask your child to hold up the appropriate hand to show how he would feel in each situation.

▶ It may be useful to think of recent happenings in your child's life to use for this activity so that you can discuss his thoughts, feelings, and behaviors in more depth.

▶ As your child takes a guess at the feeling, remember that he is just starting to understand feelings. He may guess "happy" for a time that was "sad," but you can use that time to talk with him about the meaning of those feeling words.

▶ Brainstorm words and phrases together that children can use to help them play and learn together, and write them down. Here are some suggestions:

May I play with you?

When you are finished, may I have a turn?

Please stop it. I don't like it.

Can we take turns?

Do you want to play together?

Thank you for asking me to play. I want to finish this first.

I like this. Can we do it together?

▶ Find magazine pictures or books of children with happy or sad faces, and help your child think of what might have happened in each situation. Work together to make up a pretend conversation for the sad faces, and then help your child think of a solution using the useful ideas that you've written down.

*You can download this activity and the other at-home activities in this book at www.centerforresilientchildren.org/SSES.

When We Were Little; Now That We're Big!

Helps adults learn what is developmentally appropriate for children and maintain realistic expectations for each child as an individual.

What Children Will Learn

Having the opportunity to reflect on what babies do, what we currently can do, and what we still hope to learn is a fun and insightful way for children to learn about the growth process. It is also a nice reminder for adults to celebrate every stage and milestone, knowing that there are always skills to be further developed, but making sure to reflect on how far each child has come.

Social and Emotional Skills Supported

Attachment, Initiative, and Self-Control

Materials Needed

When I Was Little by Jamie Lee Curtis (or similar story about growing up)

What to Do

▶ Ask the children to think about when they were babies. You might even ask each child to bring in a baby picture and take turns guessing which picture matches each of the children.

▶ Then, discuss as a group, "When you were a baby, what things did you probably like to do?" Make a list or draw pictures.

▶ Next, talk about what things babies cannot yet do, and are still learning.

▶ Now, talk about how old the children are today and ask the same questions: "What things do you like to do?" and "What are you still learning?"

▶ Talk about big brothers and sisters, older friends, and cousins. Are there things they can do now that you are still learning?

▶ Wrap-up with a story such as *When I Was Little* by Jamie Lee Curtis, which shares some of the fun stages of growth and development and also celebrates that we are continuing to learn and grow every day.

Social & Emotional Lenses
How quickly they grow! Know that every day is a gift and enjoy each stage!

When We Were Little; Now That We're Big

Try this activity at home to reinforce what your child learned about the growth process.

What Your Child Will Learn

Having the opportunity to reflect on what babies do, what we currently can do, and what we still hope to learn is a fun and insightful way for your child to learn about the growth process. It is also a nice reminder for you to celebrate your child's every stage and milestone, knowing that there are always skills to be further developed, but making sure to reflect on how much your child has accomplished.

Materials Needed

photographs of your child at different ages, with descriptions of how old he was and what he was doing in each photograph

When I Was Little by Jamie Lee Curtis (or similar story about growing up)

What to Do

▶ Talk to your child about when he was a baby. Ask questions such as: "When you were a baby, what things did you probably like to do?"

▶ Next, talk about what things babies cannot yet do, and are still learning.

▶ Now, talk about how old your child is today and ask the same questions: "What things do you like to do?" and "What are you still learning?"

▶ Show your child the pictures and see if he can match each age and description to the picture. Ask questions to see if your child remembers the event.

▶ End with a story such as *When I Was Little* by Jamie Lee Curtis, which shares some of the fun stages of growth and development and also celebrates that we are continuing to learn and grow every day.

*You can download this activity and the other at-home activities in this book at
www.centerforresilientchildren.org/SSES.

President for a Day!

Involves children in setting a few positively stated rules and guidelines.

What Children Will Learn

Rules help keep us safe and help us have fun while exploring and playing. When children have the chance to be a part of making the rules, they will feel more empowered and eager to follow them! When children take care of themselves, their friends, and the environment around them, they are helping foster the best opportunities for everyone to develop social and emotional skills.

Social and Emotional Skills Supported

Initiative, Self-Control

Materials Needed

crayons, markers, pencils, paper
pictures of the White House
other items related to the presidency

What to Do

- Talk with the children about the role of the President of the United States, and the role we play as citizens of this country. Help the children learn how to make "big decisions" and decide what rules they would make if they were President for a Day!
- Show pictures as you talk about the President. Encourage the children to tell you what they know about presidents.
- Explain to the children that one of the big responsibilities a president has is to help make rules (also called laws).
- Ask the children what new rules and laws they would make if they were elected. Guide the children to come up with rules that fall under these three main categories:
  - take care of ourselves
  - take care of our friends
  - take care of the place we live and learn
- Write their individual responses on paper under the caption, "If I Were President for a Day!"

Social & Emotional Lenses
Revisit your classroom rules. Could anything be adjusted to help the rules work better for you and the children?

Special Note: When forming rules for your classroom, some important guidelines include:

▶ Involving the children in deciding on the rules needed to keep everyone safe;

▶ Focusing on the main categories of safe and fun learning spaces: taking care of ourselves, taking care of each other, and taking care of our classroom and materials;

▶ Limiting the number of rules to 3–5 because children will be overwhelmed if there are too many rules; and

▶ Writing the rules in positive language, stating what the children *should* do—for example, saying, "We are kind to each other" tells the child what the expectations are versus saying, "Don't be mean."

Try this activity at home to reinforce what your child learned about making and following rules.

What Your Child Will Learn

Rules help keep us safe and help us have fun while exploring and playing. When your child has the chance to be a part of making the rules, he will feel more empowered and eager to follow them! When your child takes care of himself, his friends, and the environment, you are helping foster the best opportunities for everyone to develop social and emotional skills.

Materials Needed

art supplies

paper

pictures of the White House and the President

other items related to the presidency

What to Do

▶ Ask your child what he learned in school about the President of the United States and share pictures of the President and White House if you choose.

▶ Remind your child that one of the big responsibilities a president has is to help make rules (also called laws).

▶ Share additional information on why we need leaders and laws and rules.

▶ In general, most rules come under these three main categories:
  ◀ take care of ourselves
  ◀ take care of our friends
  ◀ take care of the place we live and learn

▶ Ask your child about the rules and laws the class came up with.

▶ Now, talk about rules you may have in your house. Talk about why you need rules at home as well as at school and in our country as a whole.

▶ Together with your child make a list of rules that everyone should follow at home, and hang it up in the house for all to see.

Special Note: When forming rules for your home, some important guidelines include:

▶ Involving children in deciding on the rules needed to keep everyone safe;

▶ Focusing on the main categories of a safe and fun home: taking care of ourselves, taking care of each other, and taking care of our home and materials;

▶ Limiting the number of rules to 3-5 because children will be overwhelmed if there are too many rules; and

▶ Writing the rules in positive language, stating what the children *should* do—"We are kind to each other" tells the child what the expectations are versus saying, "Don't be mean."

*You can download this activity and the other at-home activities in this book at
www.centerforresilientchildren.org/SSES.

That's My Name!

Supports children in building trusting relationships with caring adults.

What Children Will Learn

Most children like hearing their names used in positive and fun ways. When adults take the time to talk with each child individually, it promotes a stronger bond. Exposing children early to making personal connections through use of others' names is a great way to begin promoting social and emotional development because it gives them a secure base to help them establish trust, feel attached, and know they are safe to explore and learn new things.

Social and Emotional Skill Supported

Attachment

Materials Needed

What to Do

▸ Use the children's names and give them one-on-one attention every day to help develop their self-confidence. Whenever possible, notice something special about them, and make this a part of your greeting as well. "Good morning, Nicole. I see you put on your really fast red shoes today." "Curtis, what a nice smile you have on your face this afternoon!"

▸ Encourage the children to use the names of others they meet and interact with. Instead of just saying, "Hi" when they see a friend, we can model by using that child's name. When a child is entering a new situation, help introduce all of the children to each other, just as you would when adults are just meeting.

▸ When singing songs or reading stories, replace the characters' names with names of the children, for example, "Liz and the Three Little Pigs" or "When Amanda Gets Angry!"

▸ For an added touch, pick two or three children each day (depending on the number of children in your care) whom you will reach out to and spend special time with throughout the day. For example, you can join them in play, while reading, or when they are enjoying a snack. Remember to always ask the children first if it is okay to join them in an activity. Add the initials of these children to your lesson plan (or daily plan) to help you remember to join them in the activities they enjoy throughout the day.

Social & Emotional Lenses
Try to use the names of everyone in your life more often, with children and adults alike! Stronger connections are made when people feel noticed and special.

▶ Sing the familiar songs below, taking turns inserting the children's names.

"Stand Up" (Sung to the tune of "Frère Jacques")
Stand up, _____. Stand up, _____.
Reach up high. Reach up high.
Reach up very high, _____.
Reach up to the sky, _____.
Then sit down. Then sit down.

"Look Who's Here!" (Sung to the tune of "Twinkle, Twinkle Little Star")
_____ came to school today.
We're so glad; we'll shout "Hooray!"

"Where Is _____?" (Sung to the tune of "Frère Jacques")
Teacher: Where is (say child's name)*?*
Where is (say child's name)*?*
Child: Here I am, here I am,
Teacher: How are you today, (say child's name)*?*
Child: Very well, I thank you.
Teacher and Child: Here we are, here we are!

That's My Name!

Try this activity at home to reinforce what your child learned about building relationships and making personal connections.

What Your Child Will Learn

Exposing children early to making personal connections through use of others' names is a great way to begin promoting social and emotional development because it gives them a secure base to help them establish trust, feel attached, and know they are safe to explore and learn new things.

Materials Needed

pictures of friends and family members

What to Do

▶ Show your child the pictures of friends and family members. Ask your child to name each person.

▶ Talk with your child about his or her name, and how it was chosen.

▶ Make up a funny story together, using the people from the photographs and your child.

▶ Act out the conversation. You play the role of the person in the photograph, making sure to focus on saying your child's name.

Let Me Show You

Supports children's growing independence and competence.

What Children Will Learn

When children get to reflect on their own interests and strengths, they realize how special they really are. Adults will enjoy hearing the children talk about their unique talents, and perhaps will be able to add some that didn't occur to the children. When we take the time to focus on the positive things a child can do, there is less time to focus on the negative—making our world a much happier place.

Social and Emotional Skill Supported

Initiative

Materials Needed

Cleversticks by Bernard Ashley (or any book that has a theme of celebrating a child's unique skills and abilities)
crayons
paper

What to Do

▶ Introduce the important idea of individuality. Assure the children that although they may not be able to do everything that their brothers and sisters or peers can do, they are unique individuals with special abilities they can share.

▶ Read the book *Cleversticks* to the children.

▶ After you read this story to the children, ask:

"*How do you feel when everyone else seems to be able to do something you have not yet learned?*"

"*What is something special that you are very good at doing?*"

"*How do you think the little boy felt when he shared something special with his friends?*"

"*When he started to ask his friends for help with the things they were good at, what did he finally learn to do?*"

▶ Explain to the children that they are going to make a book of their own, highlighting the things that they enjoy and can do well.

▶ Working along with the children and using the materials you have available, create a page for each child using her name and the following statement:

"_____ is really good at _____!"

▶ Encourage the children to determine their own strengths/talents. If they are unsuccessful in doing so, use what you know about the children to help them come up with something they are good at doing. With careful observation, you should be able to find something to list next to every name (zipping coats, tying shoes, jumping really high, whistling, kicking a ball, counting to 20, saying the colors, sharing with a friend, helping friends clean up, and so on).

▶ After the children have had an opportunity to create their pages, have them draw pictures that illustrate these skills. Then, assemble the pages together to form a book they will love reading and sharing with others!

Social & Emotional Lenses
We all have things about us that make us unique. What are some of the special skills and talents you can share with others in your life?

Try this activity at home to reinforce what your child learned about her own interests and strengths.

What Your Child Will Learn

When children get to reflect on their own interests and strengths, they realize how special they really are. You can enjoy hearing your child talk about her unique talents, and you can even add some that didn't occur to your child. When we take the time to focus on the positive things a child can do, there is less time to focus on the negative—making our world a much happier place.

Materials Needed

Cleversticks by Bernard Ashley (or any book that has a theme of celebrating a child's unique skills and abilities)

crayons

paper

What to Do

▶ Begin by reading the book *Cleversticks* to your child.

▶ After you read this story, ask:

"*How do you feel when everyone else seems to be able to do something you have not yet learned?*"

"*What is something special that you are very good at doing?*"

"*How do you think the little boy felt when he shared something special with his friends?*"

"*When he started to ask his friends for help with the things they were good at, what did he finally learn to do?*"

▶ Explain that you and your child are going to make a book highlighting the things that she enjoys and can do well.

▶ Help your child create a page using her name and the following statement:
"_____is really good at _____!" Make as many pages as the child wishes.

▶ Encourage your child to determine her own strengths/talents.

▶ Now have your child draw pictures that illustrate these skills. Finally, assemble the pages together to form a book you and your child will love reading and sharing with others!

*You can download this activity and the other at-home activities in this book at
www.centerforresilientchildren.org/SSES.

28   SOCIALLY STRONG, EMOTIONALLY SECURE

Feelings Quilt

Helps children understand their feelings and those of others.

What Children Will Learn

Concepts such as "feelings" that you can't hold or touch are very difficult for young children to understand. Adding facial expressions to match the labels we give to emotions is a helpful way for children to start making connections between abstract concepts and what the feeling really looks like. As children begin to recognize emotions on their own faces, they will be much more prepared to notice and understand how others are feeling.

Social and Emotional Skills Supported

Attachment, Initiative, and Self-Control

Materials Needed

camera
construction paper
crayons
scissors

yarn or ribbon
fabric scraps (optional)
hot glue gun (optional)

What to Do

▶ Start by photographing the expressive faces and bodies of the children.

▶ Place the photographs on individual squares of construction paper. The children can help you do this.

▶ If you choose, you can use fabric scraps and hot glue the photos to the fabric scraps (adult step only).

▶ Next, ask each child how they were feeling in the picture. Point out facial expression/body language or any other clues from the photo, and then write down what the child says. "In this picture, Lydia, you have a frown on your face and tears in your eyes. How were you feeling?"

▶ Show the children how you can "read" the quilt. Point out body expressions (smiles, frowns, clenched hands, flushed faces, and so on).

▶ Call attention to the quilt regularly and add new photos when possible. Use the quilt as a reference when you are reading a story or talking about feelings, in order to help attach a visual with feeling words such as "frustrated," "angry," "disappointed," "excited," "worried," and so on. Have the quilt available for the children to look at by themselves, with an adult, or with a friend.

NOTE: This activity requires advance preparation to capture the many "faces" of the children. Ask each child to "pose" for you with various facial expressions such as: happy, excited, sad, angry, worried, frustrated, confused, and so on. Remember, not all children are comfortable having their pictures taken. You can modify this activity by having those children draw pictures of the ways they feel.

Social & Emotional Lenses

Our faces and bodies say so much! Remember, you are a role model of facial expressions and body language for the children!

Try this activity at home to reinforce what your child learned about recognizing emotions in himself and others.

What Your Child Will Learn

Concepts such as "feelings" that you can't hold or touch are very difficult for young children to understand. Adding facial expressions to match the labels we give to emotions is a helpful way for your child to start making connections between abstract concepts and what the feeling really looks like. As your child begins to recognize emotions on his own face, he will be more prepared to notice and understand how others are feeling.

Materials Needed

camera	crayons	yarn or ribbon
construction paper	scissors	

What to Do

▶ Start by photographing your child displaying a variety of feelings. You can ask your child to "pose" for you and try to capture feelings such as: happy, excited, sad, angry, worried, frustrated, confused, and so on.

▶ Place the photographs on individual squares of construction paper. Your child can help you do this. If you choose, you can use fabric scraps and hot glue the photos to the fabric scraps (adult step only).

▶ Next, ask your child how he was feeling in each picture. Point out facial expression/body language or any other clues from the photo, and then write down what your child says. "In this picture, Sam, you have a frown on your face. How were you feeling?"

▶ Consider adding other family members and their facial expressions, as well.

▶ Show your child how you can "read" the quilt. Point out body expressions (smiles, frowns, clenched hands, flushed faces, and so on).

▶ Call attention to the quilt regularly and add new photos when possible. Use the quilt as a reference when you are reading a story or talking about feelings, in order to help attach a visual with "feeling" words, such as "frustrated," "angry," "disappointed," "excited," "worried," and so on. Have the quilt available for your child to look at by himself, with an adult, or with a friend.

*You can download this activity and the other at-home activities in this book at
www.centerforresilientchildren.org/SSES.

30   SOCIALLY STRONG, EMOTIONALLY SECURE

Puppet Talk

Attempts to explore the reasons behind behavior, understanding that children will use challenging behaviors until we teach them to find more appropriate and acceptable ways to get their needs met.

What Children Will Learn

Acting out scenes that are either make-believe or loosely based on children's own lives helps them work through the beginnings of conflict-resolution, or simply stated, they start to understand how to solve problems. Children use behaviors for a reason. Adults who are observing children closely in dramatic play may begin to see these

roots of behavior played out in the stories children tell. Pay close attention to begin to help children become life-long problem-solvers!

Social and Emotional Skills Supported

Attachment, Initiative, and Self-Control

Materials Needed

craft sticks

crayons

markers

old magazines

old socks

paper plates

tape

What to Do

▶ Using the materials you have available, make a puppet with the children. If you are using a paper plate, use crayons and markers to make various facial features. You can also look through magazines for decorative elements to add. After different faces have been created, tape the paper plates to craft sticks.

▶ Puppet play may be new to the children, so you might first use puppets to make up a story of your own. During your story, be sure to talk about your feelings, behaviors, and actions. The goal of this activity is to help the children to describe their own behaviors and actions.

▶ As children gain confidence in their puppet play, adults can make the stories more meaningful by talking about problem-solving between the characters. "How do you think Michael can work with Janie to solve the problem?" Getting the children started in brainstorming solutions will help when real behavioral concerns arise that must be addressed and worked through.

▶ As you find the children growing to enjoy puppet play, help them to use their homemade puppets to put on a show based on the stories they told you.

Social & Emotional Lenses

The next time you are searching for a way to understand a child's emotions, introduce puppet play and other dramatic play activities to give the child a way to communicate through play!

Try this activity at home to reinforce what your child learned about conflict-resolution and the problem-solving process.

What Your Child Will Learn

Acting out scenes that are either make-believe or loosely based on your child's own life helps him work through the beginnings of conflict-resolution, or simply stated, he starts to understand the problem-solving process. Children use behaviors for a reason. As you observe your child closely in dramatic play, you may begin to see these roots of behavior played out in the stories your child tells. Pay close attention to begin to help your child on the way to becoming a life-long problem-solver!

Materials Needed

craft sticks	old socks
crayons	paper plates
markers	tape
old magazines	

What to Do

▶ Using the materials you have available, make a few puppets with your child. If you are using paper plates, use crayons and markers to make various facial features. You can also look through magazines for decorative elements to add. After your child has drawn the faces, tape the paper plates to craft sticks. Make many different puppets with your child over time until you have a nice collection so the puppets can interact.

▶ If puppet play is new to your child, you might first use puppets to make up a story of your own. During your story, be sure to talk about your feelings, behaviors, and actions. The goal of this activity is to help your child to describe his own behaviors and actions.

▶ As your child gains confidence in his puppet play, you can make the stories more meaningful by talking about problem-solving between the characters. "How do you think these two puppets can solve this problem?" Getting your child started in brainstorming solutions will help when real behavioral concerns arise that must be addressed and worked through.

▶ Help your child use his homemade puppets to put on a show based on the stories he tells you.

*You can download this activity and the other at-home activities in this book at
www.centerforresilientchildren.org/SSES.

Family & Friendship Fruit Salad

Supports cooperation, guiding children as they learn to take turns and work together.

What Children Will Learn

Working on a task as a group can add excitement, discussion, goal-directed behaviors, collaboration, and meaning to the effort. As adults, we need to tell children specifically about what they are doing. "You are all working so nicely together taking turns, being patient, and working as a team!" These behaviors should be pointed out repeatedly when children collaborate, as we so often remind them to use these friendly behaviors when they are at play. When children feel pride in working together, they will be eager to cooperate in the future.

Social and Emotional Skills Supported

Attachment, Initiative, and Self-Control

Materials Needed

fruit	small bowls and spoons (one for
large serving bowl	each child)
plastic silverware	whipped cream

What to Do

▶ If possible, ask the children to bring in a piece of fruit from home, perhaps one of their family favorites. This allows each child the opportunity to talk about something his or her family enjoys, and also opens discussion among peers about variety and respecting others' likes and dislikes. **NOTE:** Identify any children who have food allergies or restrictions that would make serving certain fruits unsafe or inappropriate.

▶ Once you have gathered the fruit, let the children help you wash it.

▶ Using a plastic knife and small paper plate, demonstrate how to cut the fruit into small pieces.

▶ Encourage the children to cut their fruit and put it on the plate.

▶ Invite the children to add the cut up fruit to the large mixing bowl.

▶ Pass the mixing bowl around, and let the children take turns stirring the mixture. Offer specific encouragement to the children for their cooperation, being sure to talk about teamwork and taking turns together.

▶ Finally, encourage each child to get a little "Family and Friendship Fruit Salad." Add whipped cream to make it extra yummy.

Fruit Salad Options

(Be creative!)

Grapes	Mangos
Strawberries	Bananas
Oranges	Watermelon
Cantaloupe	Kiwi
Apples	Others

Social & Emotional Lenses

Preparing and cooking foods together with children is a great way to introduce teamwork and cooperation, plus the outcome is very yummy!

Family & Friendship Fruit Salad

Try this activity at home with siblings and/or friends to reinforce what your child learned about cooperation.

What Your Child Will Learn

Encourage your child to collaborate with his siblings and/or friends to accomplish this task. When your child feels pride in working together with other children, he will be eager to cooperate in the future.

Materials Needed

fruit
large serving bowl
plastic silverware
small bowl and spoon
whipped cream

What to Do

▸ Talk about fruit with your child. Make a list of his favorite kinds of fruit, and talk about where it comes from and how it grows.
▸ Take your child along to the grocery store and let him help pick out some favorite fruits.
▸ Wash, peel, and cut the fruit together.
▸ When you have cut up all the fruit, take turns putting it in the large mixing bowl and stirring it.
▸ Offer encouragement to your child for cooperating, being sure to talk about teamwork and taking turns together.
▸ Finally, encourage your child to serve himself a little "Family & Friendship Fruit Salad." Add whipped cream to make it extra yummy.

*You can download this activity and the other at-home activities in this book at www.centerforresilientchildren.org/SSES.

Negotiation Station

Teaches children problem-solving skills and encourages them to use their skills to resolve conflicts.

What Children Will Learn

A Negotiation Station is a simple way to begin to teach young children about problem-solving and empathy, two skills very much needed as we prepare them for social relationships throughout life. The process of negotiating is a complex skill. It will take time and diligent effort to support children in this process, but you are laying the groundwork for children who can solve their OWN problems in the future!

Social and Emotional Skills Supported

Attachment, Initiative, and Self-Control

Materials Needed

an area with a small table and chairs designated just for the purpose of negotiating (NOTE: Make this peaceful area your own by adding personal touches you know will help the children calm down and talk about their feelings)

"touch" closet light

vase of flowers (artificial/silk are fine)

What to Do

▶ When young children have conflicts or difficulty with others, adults often force children to say, "I'm sorry" for their behavior. A Negotiation Station is a much better approach.

▶ Introduce the children to the word "negotiate" by telling them it simply means talking things out and finding a way to solve a problem.

▶ Work with the children to determine a place for the Negotiation Station. Here are a few items for the Negotiation Station Area:
- ◀ books about emotions
- ◀ mirror to look at facial expressions
- ◀ puppets
- ◀ a box of tissues
- ◀ feeling cards (cards that display faces representing a wide range of feelings/emotions)
- ◀ pencils, crayons, markers, and paper
- ◀ friendship lotion (perfume-free, hypo-allergenic hand lotion with just a little glitter!)

NOTE: You will need to create an area in your classroom with small tables and chairs designated just for the purpose of negotiating and talking through issues.

Tell what happened.
Each child has a turn telling what happened
from his or her perspective.
Define the problem.
The children involved in the conflict define the source of the
conflict (what are the facts about what happened).
Think of other solutions.
Children decide on alternative ways to solve their problem
(with adult help, as necessary).
Try the solution.
Think about how it worked.
Try another solution
if the first one didn't work!

- ▶ When conflicts arise throughout the day, encourage the children to go to the Negotiation Station to talk about what happened.

- ▶ You will need to help the children identify who they need to talk with, and invite others to join you at the Negotiation Station.

- ▶ At first you may need to participate with the children a few times. Help them state the problem and talk about how they feel. Then help them decide on a solution.

- ▶ Once the children are in the Negotiation Station, they will signal the adult(s) (as well as other children) that they are beginning the process of negotiating by turning on the touch light placed on or near the negotiation station. (A bell or other "signal" can be used in place of the touch light.)

- ▶ Children should be given special recognition and verbal encouragement when they have visited the Negotiation Station (a smile, handshake, high five, and/or verbal encouragement: "Way to go! You helped solve your problem!").

- ▶ When leaving the Negotiation Station, the children might put on a little Friendship Lotion, just for an added touch!

Social & Emotional Lenses
Most adults could help solve a problem between children in just a few seconds. But the magic happens when adults help children learn to solve problems for *themselves*.

Negotiation Station

Try this activity at home to reinforce what your child learned about recognizing feelings in herself and others.

Materials Needed

an area with a small table and chairs designated just for the purpose of negotiating or talking about our problems and conflicts (**NOTE:** Make this peaceful area your own by adding personal touches you know will help your child calm down and talk about feelings)

"touch" closet light

vase of flowers (artificial/silk are just fine)

What to Do

▶ Introduce your child to the word "negotiate" by telling her it means talking things out and finding ways to solve problems.

▶ Find and create a Negotiation Station together with your child. Have her help you find a way to decorate it to make it comfortable. Here are a few items that can be used in the Negotiation Station:

- ◂ books about emotions
- ◂ mirror to see how she feels
- ◂ puppets
- ◂ a box of tissues
- ◂ feeling cards (cards that display faces representing a wide range of feelings/emotions)
- ◂ pencils, crayons, markers, and paper
- ◂ friendship lotion (perfume-free, hypo-allergenic hand lotion with just a little glitter!)

▶ When a conflict arises, encourage your child to go to the Negotiation Station to talk about what happened. You will need to go with her at first to help her state the problem, how she feels, what a good solution might be. When friends or young family members come over to play, explain to them what the Negotiation Station is, and encourage them to use it, too.

▶ Your child should not have to ask for your permission to go to the Negotiation Station; however, she should let you know (as well as other children that might be over) that she is beginning the process of negotiating by turning on the touch light placed on or near the negotiation station. (A bell or other "signal" can be used in place of the touch light.)

▶ Give your child special recognition and verbal encouragement for visiting the Negotiation Station (a smile, handshake, high five, and/or verbal encouragement: "I liked the way you talked to me about your problem!").

▶ When leaving the Negotiation Station, your child might put on a little Friendship Lotion, just for an added touch!

NOTE: For families who believe a "talk spot" would work in place of a "negotiation station," feel free to individualize this activity to meet your family's needs!

*You can download this activity and the other at-home activities in this book at www.centerforresilientchildren.org/SSES.

38   SOCIALLY STRONG, EMOTIONALLY SECURE

Message Center

Helps create a safe, fun, and nurturing community of caring in which children can play, work, and learn.

What Children Will Learn

"You are wonderful!" "I hope you are feeling better!" "You are my friend!" These are just the sorts of greetings the children might share using their "Message Center." Children learn that it feels good to get messages from other children and adults, and it feels good to tell others how much we care and enjoy their company, as well!

Social and Emotional Skills Supported

Attachment and Initiative

Materials Needed

crayons, markers, pencils,
  construction/wrapping paper,
  and other decorative items

paper
shoe box
small envelopes (optional)

What to Do

▸ Invite the children to decorate the shoe box with you. Cover it with wrapping paper, construction paper, or contact paper.

▸ Include a small opening in the lid for the children to drop their notes.

▸ Set up the message center with art materials (e.g., pencils, crayons, markers) for writing notes and/or drawing pictures.

▸ Encourage the children to "write" and send greetings to one another.

▸ Adults can also send special messages to the children. What a wonderful way to show you care!

▸ Make sure the messages get delivered by choosing one child each day to be the delivery person. This person is responsible for picking up the messages from the box and delivering them to the children and adults in the classroom.

Social & Emotional Lenses

Attachment is a key protective factor and social and emotional skill that children need to be successful in school and in life! Learn more about this protective factor at www.devereuxearly childhood.org

Try having a "Message Center" at home to make your child feel special!

Materials Needed

crayons, markers, pencils, construction/wrapping paper, and other decorative items

paper

shoe box

small envelopes (optional)

What to Do

▸ Invite your child to decorate the shoe box with you. The shoe box can be covered with wrapping paper, construction paper, or contact paper. Don't forget to cut a small opening in the lid so that family members and friends can drop their notes into the box.

▸ Set up the message center with art materials (e.g. pencils, crayons, markers) for writing notes and/or drawing pictures.

▸ Encourage your child to "write" and send greetings to you and other family members. Respond to each message to show that you care!

*You can download this activity and the other at-home activities in this book at
www.centerforresilientchildren.org/SSES.

40   SOCIALLY STRONG, EMOTIONALLY SECURE

Promoting Resilience Through Home and School Partnerships

Good relationships between teachers and families are important in order for children to succeed. Teachers and families have an impact on children in a special way. When these positive efforts are combined, teachers and families can work as a team to help a child. Wonderful, supportive relationships between school and home can form when we each rethink our own role. In the classroom, if we think of our role as not simply caring for and educating children, but as helping families get off to the right start, then our goals change. As parents, we should think of our role as the first, most important and long-lasting teacher our children will have. When teachers and families work together to share their knowledge and expertise, they form a partnership to help each child grow, learn, and succeed!

What Research Says

In an encouraging classroom, teachers build partnerships with families in order to bridge differences between home and school and to enhance the home-school connection. These teachers recognize that how they respond to the child's family affects the behavior of the child at school (Gartrell, 2004).

Programmatic success is clearly reliant, in great measure, on the extent to which families participate in the programs designed to serve them (Brooks-Gunn et al., 2000). The extent to which families help create and maintain a strong "bridge" between home and school communication and collaboration helps promote goal attainment for their child or children (Espinosa, 2010).

Through positive parent/teacher relationships, teachers can better learn about the child's interests, needs and abilities (Barrera, Corso & Macpherson, 2003).

What's Ahead

In this chapter, you will find everyday strategies that can be used to strengthen school and home partnerships as well as build key social and emotional skills in children. Three key social and emotional skills that will be highlighted are: initiative, attachment, and self-control. When you use strategies that focus on school and home partnerships, you support:

▶ Children's **initiative**. Teachers have an understanding of child development and knowledge of the child in the group. Families have

in-depth information about their children and their home activities and behaviors. Both perspectives are needed to successfully encourage children to become more independent and use their own thoughts and actions to meet their needs.

▶ Children's **attachment.** When teachers and families form a partnership, children see the important adults in their lives working together to support their development. As a result, the child can thrive and grow in both the home and school environment.

▶ Children's **self-control.** As children are learning to express emotions, handle frustrations, and solve problems, teachers and families must consider developmentally appropriate expectations. When they share knowledge with each another about how children grow and develop, they can maintain and reinforce appropriate expectations for children's behavior and respond in ways that help children learn and grow.

10 Ways to Promote Resilience Using Home and School Partnerships

1. Learn about and respect the family and culture of those important people in children's lives.

2. Celebrate what the child and her family CAN do, drawing on strengths, interests, and abilities.

3. Establish an ongoing system for exchanging information between school and home.

4. Help ensure success at home and school by breaking regular tasks and routines into smaller, more manageable steps.

5. Use a variety of strategies to ensure good communication and a partnership between school and home.

6. Encourage children to talk about school happenings and happenings at home, as both environments help shape their worlds.

7. Find and use healthy ways to reduce stress and avoid adding to the stress of others.

8. Support each child's relationship with all caring adults in her life.

9. Encourage and support children as they learn to take care of their personal items and shared items in the home and school settings.

10. In both home and school environments, model for children the skills and behaviors you hope they will learn to use themselves.

Family Show and Tell

Helps children learn about and respect the family and the culture of those important people in their lives.

What Children Will Learn

In this activity, children get to learn about the people in their lives and the lives of others. When this activity is carried out at home, children learn more about themselves, their families, and cultures. This learning sets the stage for an appreciation of other families and cultures. Children cannot learn to understand and respect other cultures until they first learn about and understand their own.

Social and Emotional Skills Supported

Attachment and Initiative

Material Needed

photos of your family and friends or family mementos, if possible

What to Do

▶ Tell each family you will be hosting a "Family Show and Tell."

▶ Have families sign up to come in on the day that best fits their schedule. Add these times and dates to your lesson plan or daily schedule.

▶ Encourage families to bring whomever they choose to Family Show and Tell. Families can also bring traditional clothing, artifacts, art, and even meals/snacks for the class to enjoy.

▶ For families who are working or who are otherwise unable to attend, ask for another "special person" in the child's life who could participate, explaining to families that you understand how busy they are, but that it is important for their child to be able to share someone special with the rest of the class.

▶ To prepare the children to receive their special classroom visitors, talk about appropriate words to use for "new" and "different" and "interesting" things they might see and hear. Encourage the children to ask questions about what they see and hear.

Social & Emotional Lenses

Remember "show and tell" when you were a child? Were you nervous, excited, a little of both? Help children prepare for this special event by asking them to talk about their feelings and continue to engage children in future discussions about their families!

Family Show and Tell

Continue to discuss your child's family and culture at home to reinforce what your child learned about respecting important people in her life.

What Your Child Will Learn

In this activity, your child will learn about the people in her life and her culture. This learning sets the stage for an appreciation of other families and cultures.

Materials Needed

art supplies

family songs, games, or traditions (optional)

labeled favorite family recipe (optional)

paper

pictures of family members

What to Do

▶ At home, mark a date on your calendar when you know family members (near and far) will be together. Events such as weddings, graduations, and family reunions present such opportunities.

▶ Gather pictures of family members that your child may or may not know. Label each picture to identify who the person is, for example "great aunt."

▶ If you know of a favorite dish or family recipe, you may want to invite your child to join you in preparing it.

▶ You may also include family songs, games, and other important traditions.

▶ It may be fun to share a story from a time when an adult in the family was the same age as your child.

▶ Before the gathering, you and your child can make a "show and tell" poster/book including all or some of the things mentioned above.

▶ At the family gathering, encourage your child to share her project.

My Family Photo Album

Celebrates what the child and family can do, drawing on strengths, interests, and abilities.

NOTE: Send a letter home to families a few days before doing this activity explaining the activity and asking families for photographs of the child's relatives–both those living nearby and those that may live far away. Be sensitive to the fact that some children may have family members who are not able to be active parts of their current lives. Also, it is important that families understand the pictures will not be returned in their original format. Suggest or offer to make photocopies or scanned images of the photos if necessary.

Social & Emotional Lenses
Think about your own family and friends. What is most important to you about those relationships?

What Children Will Learn
Children are curious about the people in their lives, and they are equally interested about "where they fit in." Have fun as you carry out this activity with the children. You may find that it promotes a sense of security for the children, knowing that they have many other adults in their lives who love and care about them.

Social and Emotional Skills Supported
Attachment, Initiative, and Self-Control

Materials Needed
5" x 7" index cards (one per picture)
contact paper (or a laminating machine)
hole punch
pictures of the children's family members
ribbon or yarn

What to Do
▸ Collect pictures of the important people and places in the children's lives. Be sure to talk about their family members who may live nearby as well as those who may live far away. Explain that family members who live far away can actually be very close when you look at pictures regularly.
▸ Give the children one index card for each picture. Have the children glue each photo to the front of an index card. Allow the photos to dry.
▸ Later in the day or on another day, help the children label the special people in their photos. Add the words to the space below the photo.
▸ Add a cover page. Punch two holes in the index cards and tie the pages together with yarn or string to make an album.
▸ If you choose to use drawings instead of actual photos, encourage the children to draw pictures representing the important people and places in their lives.

My Family Photo Album

Try this activity at home to reinforce what your child learned about family.

What Your Child Will Learn

Children are curious about the people in their lives, and they are equally interested about "where they fit in." You may find that this project promotes a sense of security for her, knowing that she has many other adults in her life who love and care about her.

Materials Needed

5" x 7" index cards (one per picture)

contact paper (or a laminating machine)

hole punch

pictures of your child's family members

ribbon or yarn

What to Do

▶ With your child, collect pictures of important people and places.

▶ Give your child one index card for each picture. Have your child glue each photo to the front of an index card. Allow the photos to dry.

▶ Later in the day or on another day, help your child write about the special people in each photo. Put this information on the back of each index card.

▶ Add a cover page. Punch two holes in the index cards and tie the pages together with yarn or string to make an album.

▶ If you choose to use drawings instead of actual photos, encourage your child to draw pictures representing the important people and places in her life.

*You can download this activity and the other at-home activities in this book at
www.centerforresilientchildren.org/SSES.

Promoting Resilience Through Home and School Partnerships

47

Pass the Message Baton

Helps adults establish an ongoing system for exchanging information between school and home.

NOTE: Children use permanent markers in this activity, so be sure to have the children protect their clothes before you begin.

What Children Will Learn

Children feel good about themselves when they know that adults have confidence in their ability to carry out tasks. In this activity, children learn that they play a role in helping build strong school and home partnerships. Their involvement in this effort will help them feel a sense of accomplishment and develop their self-esteem—two skills directly related to resilience.

Social and Emotional Skills Supported

Attachment, Initiative, and Self-Control

Materials Needed

empty tennis ball container, one per child (if you don't have access to a tennis ball container, a large envelope will do)
permanent markers
stickers

What to Do

▶ Explain to the children that together you will make a fun carrier for the special notes, schoolwork, and other information that is important to share. Show the children the container and demonstrate how notes can be rolled up and placed inside it.

▶ Give the children permanent markers in different colors.

▶ Work with the children to print their names on the empty container. Children can also add other decorative elements if they choose.

▶ You now have a creative carrier to pass information back and forth. Don't keep the baton...pass it along! Use this system to share artwork, describe home activities, share photographs, and much more.

Social & Emotional Lenses
Good news is meant to be shared! Share notes from school to home about a special or fun thing a child did or said that day.

Pass the Message Baton

Try this activity at home to reinforce what your child learned about helping play a role in building a partnership.

What Your Child Will Learn

Children feel good about themselves when they know that adults have confidence in their ability to carry out tasks. In this activity, your child will learn that she plays a role in helping build a strong system for family communication. Her involvement in this effort will help her feel a sense of accomplishment and develop her self-esteem—two skills directly related to resilience.

Materials Needed

empty container (with safe, smooth edges)
permanent markers
stickers

What to Do

▸ Explain to your child that together you will make a fun carrier for information that is important to share in the family. Show your child the container and demonstrate how notes can be rolled up and placed inside it.

▸ Provide your child with permanent markers in different colors.

▸ Work with your child to print the names of everyone in your family on the empty container. Your child can also add other decorative elements if she chooses.

▸ You now have a creative carrier for your family to use to pass information back and forth. Use this system to share papers and to let family members know when you want to make plans together!

---

*You can download this activity and the other at-home activities in this book at www.centerforresilientchildren.org/SSES.

I Can Take Care of Me

Helps focus on what is developmentally appropriate behavior for children by breaking down tasks into smaller steps to help them find success.

What Children Will Learn

Routines can seem overwhelming when they involve a number of steps. When an adult simply says "Please go clean up," a child may not know where to begin or how to complete the task. By breaking down tasks into manageable steps, a child can feels successful with each completed portion of the task. When children learn that they can do parts of a larger task, they feel more empowered to continue.

Social and Emotional Skills Supported

Attachment and Initiative

Materials Needed

camera

clear contact paper or a laminating machine

construction paper or cardboard

hole punch

What to Do

▸ Choose those personal-care routines in the children's daily schedule that they need help mastering. Try to limit process to three to five steps to help the children complete the task without becoming overwhelmed.

Examples include:

Preparing for Snack/lunch

Step 1. Wash hands.

Step 2. Sit at the table.

Step 3. Enjoy your snack/lunch.

Washing Hands

Step 1. Wet hands under warm water. Add soap.

Step 2. Rub hands together to make bubbles.

Step 3. Rub bubbles all over hands. Count to 10 three times.

Step 4. Rinse bubbles away with warm water.

Step 5. Dry hands well with a clean towel.

- ▶ After deciding on a routine, take photographs of the children carrying out each step in the routine.
- ▶ Mount the photos on cardboard, and laminate or cover them with clear contact paper to make routine cards.
- ▶ Add simple words to the pictures as a reminder of the step.
- ▶ As you help support the children in mastering this routine, go over each step using the photos and simple words.
- ▶ Mount the photos in the area where the learning is taking place or use them to make a sequence book for your classroom library.

Social & Emotional Lenses
Big tasks can become easier for young children when we help them take smaller, more manageable steps.

Try this activity at home to reinforce what your child learned about breaking down tasks into smaller steps.

What Your Child Will Learn

Routines can seem overwhelming when they involve a number of steps. When you say, "Please go clean up," your child may not know where to begin or how to complete the task. By breaking down tasks into manageable steps, your child will feel successful with each completed portion of the task. When your child learns that she can do parts of a larger task, she will feel more empowered to continue.

Materials Needed

camera

clear contact paper or a laminating machine

construction paper or cardboard

hole punch

What to Do

▶ Choose those personal-care routines in your child's daily schedule that she needs help mastering. Try to limit the steps to three to five total, to help your child complete the task without becoming overwhelmed.

Examples include:

◀ getting ready for snack/breakfast/lunch

◀ washing her hands

◀ putting on her coat or shoes

◀ brushing her teeth

◀ getting ready for bed

Washing Hands

Step 1. Wet hands under warm water. Add soap.

Step 2. Rub hands together to make bubbles.

Step 3. Rub bubbles all over hands. Count to 10 three times.

Step 4. Rinse bubbles away with warm water.

Step 5. Dry hands well with a clean towel.

▶ After deciding on a routine, take photographs of your child carrying out each step in the routine.

▶ Mount the photos on cardboard and laminate or cover them with clear contact paper to make routine cards.

▶ Add simple words to the pictures as a reminder of the step.

▶ As you help support your child in mastering this routine, go over each step using the photos you have taken.

▶ Mount the photos in the area where your child does that routine or create a book that you can review with your child.

*You can download this activity and the other at-home activities in this book at www.centerforresilientchildren.org/SSES.

The Best Messenger

Helps adults establish a strategy to ensure good communication and partnership between school and home.

What Children Will Learn

Children feel important and special when we give them tasks to complete. This activity encourages responsible behavior and teaches children how to follow directions.

Social and Emotional Skills Supported

Attachment, Initiative, and Self-Control

Materials Needed

8 ½" X 11" card stock

markers

tape (or Velcro®)

What to Do

▸ Talk with the children about how important it is that the adults in their lives know about the great things that happen both at home and in school. Let the children know that you will be giving them a "reminder bracelet" to wear when there is a special message in their book bags or back packs to share.

NOTE: Even when there is not a "special message" to share, encourage children to share happenings about their day with family members. Prompt them by saying things like, "This art project would be a great activity to talk about with your mom when she picks you up!" or, "Remember to tell your grandpa that you did the slide all by yourself today!"

▸ To create the children's "Reminder Bracelets," cut the card stock into strips approximately two inches wide.

▸ After the strips have been cut, print the words "I Have Mail" (or another caption of your choice) onto each strip.

▸ Place the reminder bracelets around the children's wrists to alert family members about the message you have placed in the child's book bag or Message Baton (see page 48).

NOTE: Send a note home to families explaining that "Reminder Bracelets" serve as a form of communication between you and them. Suggest that they write the words "Got the Message!" on the flip side of the bracelet, and have children wear the bracelets back to school the next day.

Social & Emotional Lenses
Think how special and important the children will feel when they get to be a part of the connection between their school and their home!

The Best Messenger

Try this activity at home to reinforce what your child learned about keeping good communication between school and home.

Materials Needed

8 ½" x 11" card stock

markers

Velcro® or tape

What to Do

▶ Talk to your child about why it is good to talk to her teachers and other important people in her life about the things she does at home.

▶ Explain that together, you are going to make a bracelet that will help her remember when she has something important to share with the caring adults in her life!

▶ To create your child's bracelet, cut the card stock into a thin strip approximately two inches wide.

▶ Print words on the strip that will help your child remember what she has to share:

   "I want to share something."

   "I have good news!"

   "Ask me about..." (or another caption of your choice)

▶ Use Velcro® or tape to secure the ends, making sure it is big enough to slide on and off easily.

▶ Help your child put on the bracelet when she has something important to share with others. It will help her remember!

---

*You can download this activity and the other at-home activities in this book at
www.centerforresilientchildren.org/SSES.

54   SOCIALLY STRONG, EMOTIONALLY SECURE

Bright Beginnings, Happy Endings

Encourages children to talk about school events and events at home, as both environments help shape their worlds.

What Children Will Learn

These open-ended questions require more than one-word answers and provide a starting point for good conversations. Feel free to make up your own questions to add to the lists, but remember to use questions that will allow for more than one-word answers. You want the children to know that you are interested in hearing about the experiences that took place in their day. Children enjoy talking to adults about events that happened in their lives. Letting them know that you are interested helps to build trust, and opens up communication.

Social and Emotional Skills Supported

Attachment, Initiative, and Self-Control

Materials Needed

"Bright Beginning" and "Happy Ending" Questions

What to Do

- ▶ Begin each day by asking the children one or more of the "Bright Beginning" questions below.
- ▶ End each day by asking the children one or more of the "Happy Ending" questions on the next page.
- ▶ Listen attentively as children reflect. Ask questions to help the children elaborate on the various happenings at home and school.

"Bright Beginning" Questions

- ▶ Who do you plan to play with today?
- ▶ What do you plan to play with today?
- ▶ What great things are you hoping will happen today?
- ▶ Is there anything that could happen today that would make you really, really happy?
- ▶ Is there anything that could happen today that would make you really, really sad?
- ▶ What types of things do you do at school all by yourself?
- ▶ What do you like most about school?
- ▶ What do you like least about school?
- ▶ If you get upset or angry during the day at school, what do you do to feel better?

- Tell me (show me) what you do when you want a friend to play with you.
- What do you do when you have a problem in school and need help?
- Describe for me what you plan to do at school.
- What are you looking forward to doing in school?
- What are you favorite storybooks to read at school? Why are those your favorites?
- What are the names of your best friends at school? (ask only when working one-on-one with a child)

"Happy Ending" Questions
- Who was happy at school today? Who was sad?
- What did you dream about during nap today?
- Tell me a funny story about something that happened at school today.
- I had a _____ day. What kind of day did you have? Tell me about it.
- Describe all the fun things you did today.
- What was the best part of your day today?
- I could not wait to see you today! What happened today that you want to tell me about?
- What was the most fantastic thing that happened at school today?
- Tell me about the interesting things you did at school today.
- Show me (tell me about) what you did today.
- Show me (tell me about) where you played today.
- Show me (tell me about) what you learned today.
- Talk about something that surprised you.
- Talk about something that upset you or made you angry.
- What was the friendliest thing you did for someone today?
- What was the friendliest thing someone did for you today?
- What was the kindest thing you did for someone today?
- What was the kindest thing someone did for you today?
- What did you like most about being at school today?

Social & Emotional Lenses

It's not easy to ask "open-ended" questions, but think about how much more you learn about the children when you do!

Bright Beginnings, Happy Endings

Use some of these questions at home to help your child learn to express herself and build her vocabulary.

What Your Child Will Learn

Asking your child open-ended questions helps her learn to express herself and builds her vocabulary. Open-ended questions prompt more than a "one-word" answer. For example: *What is your favorite color?* is not open-ended because it produces a one-word answer. Instead phrasing like this, *Tell me about some things that are the same color as your favorite color,* encourages more conversation with your child.

Materials Needed

"Bright Beginning" and "Happy Ending" Questions (see below)

What to Do

▸ Begin each day by asking your child one or more of the "Bright Beginning" questions below.

▸ End each day by asking your child one or more of the "Happy Ending" questions below.

▸ Listen attentively as your child reflects. Ask questions to help your child elaborate on the various happenings at home and school.

"Bright Beginning" Questions

▸ Who do you plan to play with today?

▸ What do you plan to play with today?

▸ What great things are you hoping will happen today?

▸ Is there anything that could happen today that would make you really, really happy?

▸ Is there anything that could happen today that would make you really, really sad?

▸ What types of things do you do at school all by yourself?

▸ What do you like most about school?

▸ What do you like least about school?

▸ If you get upset or angry during the day at school, what do you do to feel better?

▸ Tell me (show me) what you do when you want a friend to play with you.

▸ What do you do when you have a problem in school and need help?

▸ Describe for me what you plan to do at school.

▸ What are you looking forward to doing in school?

▸ What are the names of your best friends at school?

▸ What are you favorite storybooks to read at school? Why are those your favorites?

Continued on next page

Continued from previous page

"Happy Ending" Questions

▶ Who was happy at school today? Who was sad?

▶ What did you dream about during nap today?

▶ Tell me a funny story about something that happened at school today.

▶ I had a _____ day. What kind of day did you have? Tell me about it.

▶ Describe all the fun things you did in school today.

▶ What was the best part of your day today?

▶ I could not wait to see you today! What happened today that you want to tell me about?

▶ What was the most fantastic thing that happened at school today?

▶ Tell me about the interesting things you did at school today.

▶ Show me (tell me about) what you did today.

▶ Show me (tell me about) where you played today.

▶ Show me (tell me about) what you learned today.

▶ Talk about something that surprised you.

▶ Talk about something that upset you or made you angry.

▶ What was the friendliest thing you did for someone today?

▶ What was the friendliest thing someone did for you today?

▶ What was the kindest thing you did for someone today?

▶ What was the kindest thing someone did for you today?

▶ What did you like most about being at school today?

You can download this activity and the other at-home activities in this book at www.centerforresilientchildren.org/SSES.

Positive Postcards

Helps children and adults brighten each other's days.

What the Child Will Learn

It only takes a minute of your time to let another person know you care. When carrying out this activity and involving children in the process, we set an excellent example of care, concern, and empathy. When we share positive postcards with children, it gives them a warm feeling in their hearts—where it matters the most.

Social and Emotional Skills Supported

Attachment, Initiative, and Self-Control

Materials Needed

5" x 7" index cards, or construction paper and scissors
pens and pencils

What to Do

▶ Use blank index cards in colors of your choice, or, cut up construction paper into card-sized portions.

▶ As a regular part of your week, take some time to write and send a special note to someone who has done something positive, needs an encouraging word, or whom you wish to thank.

▶ In addition to sending the notes to the children and the family members of the children in your class, you might also include colleagues, family members, and friends.

▶ Tell the children about what you do to help brighten other people's days. Then, invite them to participate.

▶ Let the children choose who to "write" to and the materials they would like to use to decorate their cards. Help them write what they would like to say, or, write their words for them.

Social & Emotional Lenses
Whose day can YOU brighten today?

Positive Postcards

Try this activity at home to reinforce what your child learned about supporting others and making them feel loved and appreciated.

Materials Needed

5" x 7" index cards
pens and pencils

What to Do

▶ Use blank index cards in colors of your choice, or cut up construction paper into card-sized portions.

▶ Work together with your child to help her draw a picture or "write" a special note to someone who has done something positive, needs an encouraging word, or who you or your child wish to thank.

▶ Talk with your child about what you do to help brighten other people's days. Come up with ideas about ways you might do this together, such as making a meal for a family in need or offering to help in other ways.

▶ Finally, you may also want to use Positive Postcards to brighten the day of your own child. Tell your child in words how happy and proud you are to be her parent. Say "I love you" with a postcard full of Xs and Os.

*You can download this activity and the other at-home activities in this book at
www.centerforresilientchildren.org/SSES.

60   SOCIALLY STRONG, EMOTIONALLY SECURE

A Kiss I Can Keep

Helps support each child's relationship with all the caring adults in her life.

What Children Will Learn

You can help children feel loved and cared for by sharing special times together as in this outlined activity. This special bond not only smoothes transitions and moments of separation, it helps children to develop skills necessary to bond with significant others in their lives.

Social and Emotional Skills Supported

Attachment, Initiative, and Self-Control

Materials Needed

a rubber stamp or a heart cut from construction paper
The Kissing Hand by Audrey Penn

What to Do

▸ In a story rich in experiences related to separation, anxiety, and love, *The Kissing Hand* will help you introduce the children to a timeless message: When we have to be apart, our love will make us feel close by.

▸ Share the story with the children.

▸ After reading the story, engage the children in a discussion using a few of these open-ended questions:

"Do you remember your first day of school?"

"How did you feel about starting school?"

"How do you think your mommy and daddy felt when you went to school for the first time?"

"If there was a new student in our class, how could you make him/her feel more comfortable and welcome?"

▸ Conclude this activity by placing a special kiss in the palm of the children's hands. You can use a rubber stamp, a heart cut from construction paper, or another method you find appropriate.

Note: Although this story is about the first few days of school, the message can be applied to any time a child needs to be apart from someone he or she loves.

Social & Emotional Lenses

Pair this activity with the children's song, "I Keep a Kiss in My Pocket" by David Kisor, available for download from Growing Sound at http://shop.childreninc.org/song-kiss-pocket-p-18.html.

A Kiss I Can Keep

Try this activity at home to reinforce what your child learned about feeling loved and relationships with others.

What Your Child Will Learn

You can help your child feel loved and cared for by sharing special times together as in this outlined activity. This special bond not only smoothes transitions and moments of separation, it helps your child develop skills necessary to bond with significant others in her life.

Materials Needed

a rubber stamp or a heart cut from construction paper
The Kissing Hand, by Audrey Penn (or other book about being apart from someone you love)

What to Do

▶ Whether you are reading the story with your child or just talking together, the following are some ideas to spark discussion about how you and your child feel and cope when you need to be apart from each other.

▶ Engage your child in a discussion using a few of these open-ended questions and discussion points:

   "What do you remember about your first day of school?"

   "How did you feel about starting school?"

   "How do you think I felt when you went to school for the first time?"

   "When we have to be away from each other, how do you feel?"

   "This is how I feel when we have to be apart from each other…"

   "What are some ways we can feel close to each other, even when we are not together?

▶ End this activity by placing a special kiss in the palm of your child's hand. You can use a rubber stamp, a heart cut from construction paper, or another method you find appropriate.

▶ The kiss will stay with your child, even when you cannot be together. Setting up a good-bye ritual with your child will help you feel close and make the separation easier for each of you.

*You can download this activity and the other at-home activities in this book at
www.centerforresilientchildren.org/SSES.

Responsibility Apple Tree

Helps adults encourage and support children as they learn to take care of their personal items and shared items.

What Children Will Learn

The word responsible can be a "big" word for children to understand. However, when adults help children to see what responsible behaviors look like, they soon learn to understand what the word means and, more important, how to carry out such behaviors themselves. By providing children with a visual, this activity helps children to see how their responsible behaviors can create growth in themselves, friends, family, and even a tree!

Social and Emotional Skills Supported

Attachment, Initiative, and Self-Control

Materials Needed

colored construction paper
large brown paper

What to Do

▶ Introduce the word "responsibility" as "taking care of ourselves and each other," "being kind to each other," "helping," "caring for our classroom and materials," and so on.

▶ Help the children understand that in their class, the responsibility tree will grow if they help take care of themselves, each other, and their classroom.

▶ Invite the children to help you trace and cut a tree shape, branches, and apples from the colored paper.

▶ Explain that the Responsibility Apple Tree will grow new apples each time they demonstrate responsible behavior.

▶ It is a good idea to have a basket of pre-cut apples readily available to record the great "growing" that is sure to take place.

▶ Each time you see one or more of the children act responsibly, reward them by adding a new apple to the Responsibility Apple Tree. Write the friendly behavior on the apple tree (no names are necessary). Be sure to talk to the children about what happened to help the Apple Tree grow.

▶ To let children know responsible behavior is not just for them, encourage the children to add apples to the tree when they see adults, peers, and others in their environment showing responsible behavior.

NOTE: A great song to share during this activity is "Three Rules" available for download by visiting: http://shop.childreninc.org/song-three-rules-p-97.html. The lyrics of this song can be used to give children examples of responsible behaviors that fall under the categories of Taking Care of Ourselves, Taking Care of Our Friends, and Taking Care of Our School.

Social & Emotional Lenses
Try not to focus on negative behaviors; instead, catch children using friendly and positive behaviors!

Try this activity at home to reinforce what your child is learning about being responsible.

What Your Child Will Learn

The word responsible can be a "big" word for children to understand. However, when you help your child to see what responsible behaviors look like, she will soon learn to understand what the word means and, more important, how to carry out such behaviors herself. By providing her with a visual, this activity helps her understand how her responsible behaviors can create growth!

Materials Needed

colored construction paper

large brown paper

What to Do

▸ Introduce the word "responsibility" as meaning "taking care of ourselves and each other," "being kind to each other," "helping," "caring for our home and toys," and so on.

▸ Help your child understand that in your home, your responsibility tree will grow if we all help take care of ourselves, each other, and our home.

▸ Invite your child to help you trace and cut a tree shape, branches, and apples from the colored paper.

▸ Explain that the Responsibility Apple Tree will grow new apples each time someone in the family demonstrates responsible behavior.

▸ Each time your child acts responsibly, add a new apple to the Responsibility Apple Tree. Write the date on the apple and describe the friendly behavior.

▸ Have a basket of pre-cut apples ready to record the great "growing" that is sure to take place.

▸ To let your child know responsible behavior is not just for her, encourage her to add apples to the tree when she sees adults, siblings, and others in the home showing responsible behavior.

*You can download this activity and the other at-home activities in this book at
www.centerforresilientchildren.org/SSES.

Talking About Mistakes

Model for children the skills and behaviors you hope they will learn to use themselves.

What Children Will Learn

We all make mistakes and can learn from them. Let's teach children how not to become frustrated or overwhelmed by mistakes, but to learn from them. Children learn tenacity, determination, and gain a sense of accomplishment when adults help them to learn to overcome mistakes without losing their pride or sense of self.

Social and Emotional Skills Supported

Attachment, Initiative, and Self-Control

Materials Needed

Regina's Big Mistake by Marissa Moss (or another book with the theme of turning mistakes into successes) (optional)

What to Do

▶ Whether you are reading *Regina's Big Mistake* with the children or just talking together, the following are good discussion topics and open-ended questions to help talk with the children about making mistakes and dealing with frustration.

▶ Ask the children what "mistakes" are.

▶ Share what you think a "mistake" is (something you didn't mean to do, a mess-up, an accident, a goof, and so on).

▶ Share a time you made a mistake.

▶ Talk about how it feels to make mistakes.

▶ Talk about what you learned when you made a mistake and what you might do differently the next time you are in that situation.

▶ Ask the children how they feel when they make a mistake.

▶ Talk together about ways to deal with frustration. Some ideas might include:

  ◀ taking a break and then coming back to the situation,

  ◀ taking a deep breath or counting slowly to 10, and

  ◀ cleaning up a mess or finding a way to correct the mistake.

Social & Emotional Lenses

Initiative is a key protective factor and social and emotional skill that children need to be successful in school, and in life! You can learn more about this and other protective factors at www.devereuxearly childhood.org

Note: As children grow older and more confident, applaud their progress and encourage their attempts to:

▶ Persist with activities,

▶ Try new things,

▶ Find new ways to solve a problem,

▶ Concentrate on a task,

▶ Choose to do a task that was challenging, and

▶ Make their own decisions.

Each of the behaviors mentioned above relates directly to children's initiative. With a strong sense of initiative, children are ready to take on risks and challenges with grace and confidence.

Talking About Mistakes

Try this activity at home to reinforce what your child learned about making mistakes and learning from them.

What Your Child Will Learn

We all make mistakes and can learn from them. Your child must learn not to become frustrated or overwhelmed by mistakes, but to learn from them. Your child will gain tenacity, determination, and a sense accomplishment when you help her discover how to overcome mistakes without losing her pride or sense of self.

Materials Needed

Regina's Big Mistake by Marissa Moss (or another book with the theme of turning mistakes into successes) (optional)

What to Do

▸ Whether you are reading the story with your child or just talking together, the following are good discussion topics and open-ended questions to help talk with your child about making mistakes, and dealing with frustration.

▸ Ask the children what "mistakes" are.

▸ Share what you think a "mistake" is (something you didn't mean to do, a mess-up, an accident, a goof, and so on).

▸ Share a time you made a mistake.

▸ Talk about how it feels to make mistakes.

▸ Talk about what you learned when you made a mistake and what you might do differently the next time you are in that situation.

▸ Ask your child how she feels when she makes a mistake.

▸ Talk about ways to deal with frustration. Some ideas include:
  ◂ taking a break and then coming back to the situation,
  ◂ taking a deep breath or counting slowly to 10, and
  ◂ cleaning up a mess or finding a way to correct the mistake.

NOTE: As your child grows older and more confident, applaud her progress and encourage every attempt to:

▸ Persist with activities,

▸ Try new things,

▸ Find new ways to solve a problem,

▸ Concentrate on a task,

▸ Choose to do a task that was challenging, and

▸ Make decisions herself.

Each of the behaviors mentioned above relates directly to your child's initiative. With a strong sense of initiative, your child will be ready to take on risks and challenges with grace and confidence.

*You can download this activity and the other at-home activities in this book at www.centerforresilientchildren.org/SSES.

Promoting Resilience Through Activities and Experiences

To be prepared for school (and life), children need to be excited and curious about learning and feel confident that they can succeed. Every day, teachers and families must provide activities and experiences rich in opportunities for children to learn skills related to initiative, attachment, and self-control. These efforts do not belong in a box on a lesson plan or a week on a calendar, rather these skills must be taught with intention each and every day.

Playing While Learning

With the ever-present emphasis on the promotion of academic skill development in preschools, teachers and families alike may find it difficult to address all aspects of a child's development, which include cognitive and physical skill development as well as social and emotional development.

What Research Says

Young children learn better through experiencing an activity and observing behavior than through teacher-directed instruction (Fleer, M. ed., 1996). The most meaningful learning has its source in the child's self-initiated activities. The learning environment that supports individual differences, learning styles, abilities, and cultural values fosters confidence and curiosity in learners (Rodd. J., 1996; Greenberg, P., 1992).

Opportunities to be an active learner are vitally important for the development of motor competence and awareness of one's own body and person, the development of sensory motor intelligence, the ability and motivation to use physical and mental initiative, and feelings of mastery and successful coping (National Health and Safety Performance Standards, Second Edition, 2002).

Engaging children in meaningful play is one of the best ways to promote cognitive, language, physical, social, and emotional skills, as well as those related to resilience (Hyson, 2003). Activities and experiences that are planned with intention and designed to address all domains of learning are the catalyst to promoting environments where children grow and develop to their fullest potential.

What's Ahead

In this chapter, you will find everyday strategies that can be used to create activities and experiences that support resilience and build key social and emotional skills in children. As you consider each activity, it will become evident that building social and emotional skills is not done in isolation from other skill development. Activities might include developing literacy, fine and gross motor skills, and cognitive skills. The three key social and emotional skills that will be highlighted are: initiative, attachment, and self-control.

When you use strategies that focus on activities and experiences, you support:

▶ Children's **initiative**. Build on what children know and can do well. If for instance, children love to play with dough, start there. Provide materials and tools to expand on the play experience. Ask open-ended questions which challenge children to think about what they are doing and what the planned outcome may be.

▶ Children's **attachment**. Provide activities that link to the contexts, cultures, and relationships that are comfortable for children. They should be able to "see themselves" and "be themselves" in their play environments. This will help promote acceptance and appreciation, two feelings that will lead to stronger attachments within the classroom.

▶ Children's **self-control**. Provide activities that help children learn to accept, understand, and manage their emotions as well as teach problem-solving skills. Respond by being sensitive, responsive, and physically and emotionally available to children and teach the skills necessary to help them achieve their goals.

10 Ways to Promote Resilience Using Activities and Experiences

1. Use small groups or pairs to help children learn from each other.

2. Offer the choice of interacting with an adult during play time.

3. Provide open-ended activities that support a range of skills and interests.

4. Read and discuss books about feelings, and sing songs about emotions and kind ways to play with each other.

5. Encourage children to initiate their own activities, alone or with others.

6. Teach children relaxation techniques and ways to calm down.

7. Offer activities and experiences that encourage leadership and cooperation.

8. Create opportunities and activities that let children explore a variety of senses.

9. Offer physical activities that use large muscles and expend energy.

10. Provide many opportunities for children to build language skills by talking with children and asking them open-ended questions throughout the day.

The "Perfect Pair"

Helps children working in small groups to learn from each other.

What Children Will Learn

When children work in pairs or small groups and take turns serving as a peer model for others, each child has a chance to feel confident about what he or she can do. Social and emotional development thrives when children develop self-confidence and self-esteem and see themselves as highly regarded and appreciated by others, which all lead to increased resilience!

Social and Emotional Skills Supported

Attachment, Initiative, and Self-control

Materials Needed

empty, square tissue boxes (as many as 4)
photograph of each child (or each name written on paper)
Velcro®, glue, or tape

What to Do

▶ Take a picture of every child. (You can modify this activity by printing the child's name on a piece of paper instead of using a photograph.)

▶ On each side of one tissue box, use Velcro, glue, or tape to place the pictures of those children that would serve as strong role models for a particular skill. For example, if you were grouping children together for a cutting activity, you would place the photos of those children who have mastered this skill on each side of one of the tissue boxes.

▶ On another tissue box, place photos of the children in the class who could benefit from the support of a classmate. For example, photos of children who need support in learning how to cut would go on this second box.

▶ Add more tissue boxes to account for the number of children.

▶ Use your "perfect pair" cubes each time you wish to pair children together and/or to form small groups. To further enhance social and emotional skills, use this pairing method for children at varying levels of development with these important skills:

  ◀ Taking turns and using patience,
  ◀ Initiating play,
  ◀ Using creativity to solve a problem or create a project, and
  ◀ Showing persistence.

Note: It is important to make sure each child has an opportunity to "teach" and to "learn," so give each child a chance to share his/her strengths and a chance to benefit from those of others.

Social & Emotional Lenses
Use pairing cubes to break up "cliques" in the classroom and help the children get to know other children in the class.

The "Perfect Pair"

Try this activity at home to reinforce what your child learned about working in pairs and helping others.

What Your Child Will Learn

When your child learns how to work in pairs or small groups and take turns serving as a peer model for others, she has a chance to feel confident about what she can do. Social and emotional development thrives when your child develops self-confidence and self-esteem and sees herself as highly regarded and appreciated by others.

Materials Needed

magazines
scissors and tape
paper or cardboard

What to Do

▶ With your child or children, talk about what the word "pair" or "partner" means.

▶ Ask what kinds of things they like to do in pairs; such as reading a special book with Grandma, playing a favorite game with a cousin, or kicking a soccer ball with a friend in the neighborhood.

▶ Now, talk about other objects that go well together such as "peanut butter and jelly," "cereal and milk," "a sneaker and a sock," and so on. Ask your child to come up with ideas that make a good pair.

▶ Next, look through (child-friendly) magazines together to find objects that go well together or draw pictures instead.

▶ Glue your matching pictures side-by-side on paper or cardboard while you talk about some friends they might like to find more time to get to know.

▶ Set up a plan to invite the new friend to join your child in play, and watch as a special new pair of friends forms!

▶ As a bonus, take pictures of your child and his new friend and add them to the collage of perfect pairs.

*You can download this activity and the other at-home activities in this book at
www.centerforresilientchildren.org/SSES.

"Find Delight Now, Catch Up Later..."

Offers the choice of interacting with an adult during playtime.

What Children Will Learn

The saying goes: "I'm rocking my child, the cobwebs can wait..." Adults who interact with young children every day know that there are always things that need to "get done." Those tasks are important, but even more important is taking the time to truly find delight and enjoyment in the children. Carving out time each day to give your undivided attention either one-on-one or in small groups is so valuable for developing strong relationships with young children. When children form strong attachments with the important adults in their lives, they become more resilient.

Social and Emotional Skills Supported

Attachment, Initiative, and Self-Control

Materials Needed

kitchen timer (optional)

What to Do

▶ Each day, set some time aside to focus only on playing with the children. Build this time into a daily or weekly planner.

▶ Hold true to your word and go right to the children when it is time.

▶ If possible, get down on the floor at the children's level, and play like you are four years old; get lost in the delight of living the life of a child for a while. The children will be thrilled with your interest and you will see their faces beaming with happiness.

▶ After you play together, talk about what you did and what you enjoyed or learned. Ask the children what they enjoyed or learned. Then, make your next "date" to play.

Optional: Explain to the children that you will be free to play with them in 5 minutes, 10 minutes, 15 minutes (or whatever you consider an appropriate amount of time for your children's developmental level and age range). Let the children help you set the timer. Tell them that when the timer goes off you will be "all theirs" for playing! The purpose of using a timer and immediately stopping what you are doing when it goes off is to prevent that urge to say, "Just one more minute and I'll be over..." This helps children learn to trust that you mean what you say and will hold true to your promises.

Social & Emotional Lenses
How have you found delight in a child today?

"Find Delight Now, Catch Up Later…"

Try this activity at home to remind your child how important and loved he is, and that you always have time to spend with him.

What Your Child Will Learn

Playing as if it is the only thing you want to be doing at that moment is one of the most valuable gifts you can give your child. Your child knows when your heart is in it and when you are distracted. Really enjoying and finding delight in your child each day will make him feel loved and important.

Materials Needed

kitchen timer (optional)

What to Do

▶ Each day, plan to set some time aside to focus only on playing with your child.

▶ When that time comes, or when your child asks you to play, allow yourself the "five minute rule" to finish up a task (such as finishing the dishes, putting food away, or sweeping the floor).

▶ Hold true to your word and go right to your child when it is time.

▶ Play with your child as though you are four years old! Get lost in the delight of living the life of a child for a little while. Your child will be thrilled with your interest and you will see his face beaming with happiness.

▶ After you play together, talk about what you did and what you enjoyed or learned. Ask your child what he enjoyed or learned. Then, make your next "date" to play later in the day or the next day.

Optional: Explain to your child that you will be free to play with him in 5 minutes, 10 minutes, 15 minutes (or whatever you consider an appropriate amount of time for your child's developmental level). Let him help you set the timer. Tell him that when the timer goes off you will be "all his" for playing! The purpose of using a timer and immediately stopping what you are doing when it goes off is to prevent that urge to say, "Just one more minute and I'll be over…" This helps your child learn to trust that you mean what you say and will hold true to your promises.

*You can download this activity and the other at-home activities in this book at
www.centerforresilientchildren.org/SSES.

Our Welcome Wreath

Helps children working in small groups to learn from each other.

What Children Will Learn

This activity encourages the children involved to work in smaller groups and fosters a sense of cooperation and teamwork. You will be able to provide individualized support to help the children follow directions, share, take turns, and communicate. Making a project that demonstrates that each person is an important member of your classroom community is a nice way to show all the loving hands who live and play inside these doors.

Social and Emotional Skills Supported

Attachment and Initiative

Materials Needed

construction paper	markers
crayons	photographs of the children
glue	(optional)
heavy poster board	ribbon or yarn
hole punch	scissors

What to Do

▸ Cut the poster board into a large circle. Cut another circle in the middle to make the wreath shape.

▸ Invite the children to place one of their hands on construction paper, and have an adult trace the outlines of their hands.

▸ Encourage the children to cut along the outlines of their hands.

▸ Each adult in the class should also trace and cut out his/her own hand, or ask the children to help with this step.

▸ Glue the hand cutouts around the wreath. If you wish, you can add photographs and names of the adults and children to the wreath.

▸ Punch a hole in the top of the wreath, place a string or ribbon through the hole, and place the wreath on the entrance door to your classroom.

Social & Emotional Lenses
Children gain social skills when they collaborate with their peers and emotional skills when their work is validated. What are some other opportunities you can give children to collaborate?

Our Welcome Wreath

Try this activity at home to reinforce what your child learned about following directions, sharing, and communicating.

What Your Child Will Learn

This activity fosters a sense of cooperation and teamwork. Making a project that represents the important members of your family is a nice way to show all the loving hands that live and play inside these doors.

Materials Needed

construction paper

crayons

glue

heavy poster board

hole punch

markers

photographs of your child and other family members (optional)

ribbon or yarn

scissors

What to Do

▶ Cut the poster board into a large circle. Cut another circle in the middle to make the wreath shape.

▶ Invite your child to place one hand on construction paper and trace the outline.

▶ Help your child cut out the outline of his hand.

▶ Trace and cut out your own hand, or ask your child to help you.

▶ Glue the hand cutouts around the wreath. If you like, you can add photographs of your child and other family members to the wreath.

▶ As a nice touch, ask every friend and family member who comes over to add their own hand to the wreath, making it represent all loved ones who enter your door. These also make great gifts for grandparents and other family members!

▶ Punch a hole in the top of the wreath, place a string or ribbon through the hole, and place the wreath on the entrance door to your home.

*You can download this activity and the other at-home activities in this book at
www.centerforresilientchildren.org/SSES.

Turn That Frown Upside Down

Use stories, pictures, songs and open-ended questions to help children understand their feelings.

What Children Will Learn

The experience of sharing a book together benefits a child's social and emotional development, as well as literacy and pre-reading skills. Open-ended questions about any book help children learn to think, problem-solve, and relate topics to events in their own lives.

Social and Emotional Skills Supported

Attachment, Initiative, and Self-Control

Materials Needed

Badger's Bad Mood by Hiawyn Oram (or another book that explores characters' feelings)

feeling photos, downloadable from the Devereux Early Childhood Initiative website (http://www.devereux.org/site/DocServer/PreSchool-EmotionPhotos.pdf?docID=5981)

What to Do

- Explain to the children that sometimes when we are feeling down, a person who cares a lot about us can help us work through our bad mood.
- Read the story, *Badger's Bad Mood* (or a similar story).
- Ask the children these open-ended questions:
  - "Have you ever been in a bad mood? How did you act?"
  - "What helped you get out of your bad mood?"
  - "What can we do to help our friends and family members feel better when they are in a bad mood?"
  - "Have you told someone lately that you love and appreciate something they do for you?"
  - "How did that make them feel?"
- Use the feeling pictures downloadable from the DECI website.
- Ask the children to identify how they think each character felt during different parts of the story: Badger (sad), Squirrel and Rabbit (angry, offended), and Mole (sad at first, then overwhelmed, hopeful, relieved, and finally happy). Point out that in the end Badger feels appreciated, proud, and happy again.
- After reading the story, make a list of something you appreciate about every child in the classroom. Make all of the children certificates or medals that say what you appreciate about them, or simply write each child a little note.

Don't Flip Out,
Just Use FLIP IT!

Teachers and families alike can use this simple four-step process, known as FLIP IT, with children of all ages when they are angry, feeling upset, or need to work through a problem or conflict with someone.

F—FEELINGS: Ask or help identify what the child is feeling.

L—LIMITS: State the rule or expectation in a positive way, when possible.

I—INQUIRIES: Ask open-ended questions to help the child think of solutions.

P—PROMPTS: When the child seems stuck, offer some solutions.

Here is an example:

> *Two friends both grab the last cookie from the snack tray and then start pushing and arguing over who gets to eat it. The teacher intervenes using FLIP IT.*

F—"What are you each feeling?"
One child responds: "Mad!"
The other child responds: "Frustrated!"

L—"You two both really want this cookie and it is making you feel mad and frustrated. We use our hands in kind ways."

I—"What could you do instead of pushing and shouting that would help you work this out?"
Each child has a chance to respond, and if they can agree on a solution, then go with it! If they need some assistance coming up with a fair solution, move to prompts:

P—"Perhaps, one of you could use the plastic knife to cut the cookie, and the other could be the one to choose the first piece?"

Remember the steps of FLIP IT whenever you face a challenging behavior!

Rachel Sperry, MSW, is an Early Childhood Mental Health Specialist and Trainer for the Devereux Early Childhood Initiative, and the author of FLIP IT. Training and Resources are available on FLIP IT. Please visit: www.devereuxearlychildhood.org

Social & Emotional Lenses
Try this song for helping children work through a bad mood: "I Get Angry" by David Kisor, available for download from Growing Sound's website: http://shop.childreninc.org/song-get-angry-p-50.html.

Turn That Frown Upside Down

Try this technique to help your child learn to recognize and work through strong feelings in herself and others.

What Your Child Will Learn

Children's books and music about feelings help your child begin to understand and label feelings. The experience of sharing a book together benefits your child's social and emotional development, as well as literacy and pre-reading skills. Open-ended questions about any book help your child learn to think, problem solve, and relate topics to what is going on or has happened in her own life. She learns to make meaning through stories, and discussing books about feelings is a wonderful way to help her develop and grow.

Materials Needed

Badger's Bad Mood by Hiawyn Oram (optional)

feeling photos, downloadable from the Devereux Early Childhood Initiative website

(http://www.devereux.org/site/DocServer/PreSchool-EmotionPhotos.pdf?docID=5981er exact link here)

What to Do

▶ Explain to your child that sometimes when we are feeling down, a person who cares a lot about us can help us work through our bad mood.

▶ Read the story, *Badger's Bad Mood* (or a similar story).

▶ Ask your child these open-ended questions:

    ◀ "Have you ever been in a bad mood? How did you act?"

    ◀ "What helped you get out of your bad mood?"

    ◀ "What can we do to help our friends and family members feel better when they are in a bad mood?"

    ◀ "Have you told someone lately that you love and appreciate something they do for you?"

    ◀ "How did that make them feel?"

▶ Use the feeling pictures downloadable from the DECI website.

▶ Ask your child to identify how she thinks each character felt during different parts of the story: Badger (sad), Squirrel and Rabbit (angry, offended), and Mole (sad at first, then overwhelmed, hopeful, relieved, and finally happy). Point out that in the end Badger feels appreciated, proud, and happy again.

▶ After reading the story, make a list of all of the things you appreciate about your child. Make her a certificate or medal that says what you appreciate about her, or simply write your child a little note.

*You can download this activity and the other at-home activities in this book at
www.centerforresilientchildren.org/SSES.

80   SOCIALLY STRONG, EMOTIONALLY SECURE

Our Parade of Flags

Encourages children to initiate their own activities, alone or with others.

What Children Will Learn

Get ready for a parade, and don't forget your flag! This activity allows children to work independently at first, and then join the group for a social bonding experience. It also creates a meaningful opportunity for self-expression and strengthens language skills. Parading around with friends to show off their special creations will help children's self-esteem flourish, which is an important part of strong social and emotional health.

Social and Emotional Skills Supported

Attachment and Initiative

Materials Needed

crayons	glue
creative art materials (pipe cleaners, pom-poms, glitter, and so on)	markers
	paper
	scissors
empty paper towel roll (1 per child), or craft sticks	

What to Do

▶ Let each child work independently to make and decorate a flag that represents who they are, things they enjoy doing, drawings of family members, favorite colors, and so on.

▶ When the children have finished their flags, attach them to the empty paper towel rolls.

▶ When all the flags have been assembled, give each child the opportunity to talk about his flag and why he created it in his unique way.

▶ Finally, invite the children to line up for a parade through the classroom or school.

Social & Emotional Lenses
An activity like this actually promotes development across all domains for social and emotional skills, fine and gross motor skills, cognitive skills, self-help skills, and language skills.

Our Parade of Flags

Try this activity at home to reinforce what your child learned about how his self-confidence can be boosted by expressing himself freely.

What Your Child Will Learn

This activity gives your child a chance to express himself and strengthen his language skills. Parading around the home, backyard, park, neighborhood, or other special place with you to show off his special creation will help his self-esteem flourish, which is an important part of strong social and emotional health.

Materials Needed

crayons

creative art material (pipe cleaners, pom-poms, glitter, and so on)

empty paper towel roll

glue

markers

paper

scissors

What to Do

▶ Encourage your child to make a flag that represents who he is, things he enjoys doing, drawings of family members, favorite colors, and so on.

▶ Provide your child with a variety of creative art materials, and let him decorate his flag any way he likes.

▶ When your child has finished his flag, attach it to the empty paper towel roll.

▶ Take your child for a walk through the house, backyard, park, or neighborhood and let him display his flag for all to see!

*You can download this activity and the other at-home activities in this book at
www.centerforresilientchildren.org/SSES.

Turn That Frown Upside Down

Try this technique to help your child learn to recognize and work through strong feelings in herself and others.

What Your Child Will Learn

Children's books and music about feelings help your child begin to understand and label feelings. The experience of sharing a book together benefits your child's social and emotional development, as well as literacy and pre-reading skills. Open-ended questions about any book help your child learn to think, problem solve, and relate topics to what is going on or has happened in her own life. She learns to make meaning through stories, and discussing books about feelings is a wonderful way to help her develop and grow.

Materials Needed

Badger's Bad Mood by Hiawyn Oram (optional)

feeling photos, downloadable from the Devereux Early Childhood Initiative website
(http://www.devereux.org/site/DocServer/PreSchool-EmotionPhotos.pdf?docID=5981er exact link here)

What to Do

▶ Explain to your child that sometimes when we are feeling down, a person who cares a lot about us can help us work through our bad mood.

▶ Read the story, *Badger's Bad Mood* (or a similar story).

▶ Ask your child these open-ended questions:

  ◀ "Have you ever been in a bad mood? How did you act?"

  ◀ "What helped you get out of your bad mood?"

  ◀ "What can we do to help our friends and family members feel better when they are in a bad mood?"

  ◀ "Have you told someone lately that you love and appreciate something they do for you?"

  ◀ "How did that make them feel?"

▶ Use the feeling pictures downloadable from the DECI website.

▶ Ask your child to identify how she thinks each character felt during different parts of the story: Badger (sad), Squirrel and Rabbit (angry, offended), and Mole (sad at first, then overwhelmed, hopeful, relieved, and finally happy). Point out that in the end Badger feels appreciated, proud, and happy again.

▶ After reading the story, make a list of all of the things you appreciate about your child. Make her a certificate or medal that says what you appreciate about her, or simply write your child a little note.

*You can download this activity and the other at-home activities in this book at www.centerforresilientchildren.org/SSES.

Don't Flip Out,
Just Use FLIP IT!

Teachers and families alike can use this simple four-step process, known as FLIP IT, with children of all ages when they are angry, feeling upset, or need to work through a problem or conflict with someone.

F—FEELINGS: Ask or help identify what the child is feeling.

L—LIMITS: State the rule or expectation in a positive way, when possible.

I—INQUIRIES: Ask open-ended questions to help the child think of solutions.

P—PROMPTS: When the child seems stuck, offer some solutions.

Here is an example:

Two friends both grab the last cookie from the snack tray and then start pushing and arguing over who gets to eat it. The teacher intervenes using FLIP IT.

F—"What are you each feeling?"
One child responds: "Mad!"
The other child responds: "Frustrated!"

L—"You two both really want this cookie and it is making you feel mad and frustrated. We use our hands in kind ways."

I—"What could you do instead of pushing and shouting that would help you work this out?"
Each child has a chance to respond, and if they can agree on a solution, then go with it! If they need some assistance coming up with a fair solution, move to prompts:

P—"Perhaps, one of you could use the plastic knife to cut the cookie, and the other could be the one to choose the first piece?"

Remember the steps of FLIP IT whenever you face a challenging behavior!

Rachel Sperry, MSW, is an Early Childhood Mental Health Specialist and Trainer for the Devereux Early Childhood Initiative, and the author of FLIP IT. Training and Resources are available on FLIP IT. Please visit: www.devereuxearlychildhood.org

Social & Emotional Lenses
Try this song for helping children work through a bad mood: "I Get Angry" by David Kisor, available for download from Growing Sound's website:
http://shop.childreninc.org/song-get-angry-p-50.html.

Relaxation in a Bottle

Teaches children relaxation techniques and ways to calm down.

What Children Will Learn

This hands-on relaxation activity helps children begin to develop skills for self-regulation and learn how to move from an excited state to a more calm state.

Social and Emotional Skills Supported

Initiative and Self-Control

Materials Needed

clear, empty plastic bottles
    with lids (one per child;
    water bottles work best)
food coloring
glitter
heavy tape

marbles
sequins
Super Glue® (adult use only)
vegetable oil
water

What to Do

▶ Before you begin this activity, be sure to talk to the children about the need to rest our bodies from time to time. Ask the children questions about how they feel when they are relaxed. Ask them about ways they relax and settle down when they are excited.

▶ Share that this activity will give them a fun way to help them relax.

▶ Help each child fill an empty bottle ⅔ full of water.

▶ Add a few drops of food coloring. (Red, blue, green, and purple work best.)

▶ Fill the remaining space in the bottle with vegetable oil.

▶ Add sequins, marbles, and/or glitter.

▶ Glue the cap to the bottle and wrap it securely with heavy tape (adult step only).

▶ Encourage the children to swirl, shake, and spin their water bottles as a technique to help calm them. Encourage them to breath deeply.

▶ Talk children through the process of relaxation by asking them to make their marbles move very slowly from end-to-end and then to make them stop altogether.
SAFTEY NOTE: Do not allow children to chew on this bottle.

Social & Emotional Lenses
List healthy ways that YOU relax and calm down. Remember, you are a role model of strong social and emotional health to the children—take good care of yourself!

Relaxation in a Bottle

Try this activity at home to reinforce what your child learned about using a relaxation technique to calm himself down.

What the Child Will Learn
This hands-on relaxation activity helps your child begin to develop skills for self-regulation and learn how to move from an excited state to a more calm state.

Materials Needed

clear, empty plastic bottle with lid (a water bottle works well)	marbles
	sequins
food coloring	Super Glue® (adult use only)
glitter	vegetable oil
heavy tape	water

What to Do

▶ Before you begin this activity, be sure to talk to your child about the need to rest our bodies from time to time. Ask your child about how he feels when he is relaxed. Ask about ways to relax and settle down when excited.

▶ Share that this activity will provide a fun way to help calm excited bodies down, and learn to relax.

▶ Help your child fill an empty bottle ⅔ full of water.

▶ Invite him to add a few drops of food coloring. (Red, blue, green, and purple work best.)

▶ Fill the remaining space in the bottle with vegetable oil.

▶ Encourage your child to add sequins, marbles, and/or glitter.

▶ Glue the cap to the bottle and wrap it securely with heavy tape (adult step only).

▶ Encourage him to swirl, shake, and spin the water bottle as a technique to help calm him. Remember to encourage deep breathing, as well.

▶ Talk your child through the process of relaxation by asking him to make the marbles in the bottle move very slowly from end-to-end and then to make them stop altogether.

▶ SAFTEY NOTE: Do not allow your child to chew on this bottle.

*You can download this activity and the other at-home activities in this book at
www.centerforresilientchildren.org/SSES.

Follow Your Leader

Offers activities and experiences that encourage leadership and cooperation.

What the Child Will Learn

Letting a child have a chance to be the leader helps promote initiative. Some children may love being in charge, while others prefer just to watch the activity. It is appropriate to respect what each child may be feeling and to allow each to participate as they wish. Whether participating or just watching this activity, children will learn about important aspects of being a leader as well as learning to follow directions.

Social and Emotional Skills Supported

Attachment, Initiative, and Self-Control

Materials Needed

15 index cards—Prepare the cards as follows:

▶ Label five cards with an "A" on one side, five cards with a "B," and five cards with a "C."

▶ On the back of each "A" card, write the name of an object in your classroom, such as a "ball," "block," "doll," "crayon," "truck" (or any five small-to-medium-sized objects).

- On the back of each "B" card, write the name of a location on the body, such as "on your head," "on your belly," "between your knees," "in your hands," and "under your chin."
- On the back of each "C" card, write an action, such as "hop," "walk forward," "crawl," "slither on your belly," and "walk backward."

What to Do

- Talk with the children about what a leader does. Ask them, "What makes a good leader?" Encourage the children to talk about a leader being "kind and helpful."
- Choose a leader, and assure the children that they can take turns being the leader.
- The leader chooses a "A," "B," and "C" card from the pile.
- Help the child determine what action to take based on the three cards. For example, if the child chooses "block," "under your chin," and "hop," then the child must find a block, place it under his chin, and hop around the room!
- To involve all the children and make this child the leader, invite all of the children to follow the leader around the room performing the action only (all children hop behind the child with the block under his chin).
- At the end, all the children clap, and the child (or teacher) chooses the next leader.
- To add a challenge, include more cards in the game.

Social & Emotional Lenses

It is never too early to help children learn to be good leaders.

Follow Your Leader

Try this activity at home to reinforce what your child learned about being a leader and following directions. Remind your child that a leader is kind and helpful, and that we ALL need to follow directions and rules—even as parents!

Materials Needed

15 index cards—Prepare the cards as follows:

▶ Label five cards with a "A" on one side, five cards with a "B," and five cards with a "C."

▶ On the back of each "A" card, write the name of an object in your home, such as a "ball," "block," "doll," "crayon," "truck" (or any five small-to-medium-sized objects).

▶ On the back of each "B" card, write the name of a location on the body, such as "on your head," "on your belly," "between your knees," "in your hands," and "under your chin."

▶ On the back of each "C" card, write an action, such as "hop," "walk forward," "crawl," "slither on your belly," and "walk backward."

What to Do

▶ Ask your child to be the leader.

▶ The leader chooses a "A," "B," and "C" card from the pile.

▶ Help your child read what the three cards are asking him to do. For example, if your child chooses "block", "under your chin", and "hop", then he gets to go find a block, put it under his chin, and hop around the room!

▶ To involve any other children who may wish to play, have each child follow the leader around the room performing the action only (invite them to hop behind your child with the block under his chin).

▶ Now, move on to the next leader!

Our Classroom Flag

NOTE: No matter if 2 children or 20 will be participating in this activity, it is best to paint the feet of one child at a time, then wash off, then move to the next child!

Creates opportunities and activities that let children explore a variety of senses.

What Children Will Learn

Children need to understand that they are a part of a larger community. As you work together on a collaborative task such as this, there are many opportunities to talk about how many hands and feet can come together to do good things! Talk about volunteering, serving, and helping others in need, and even working together to clean up and keep our play places safe! Children's social and emotional skills will continue to thrive as you celebrate each individual, while also focusing on the strength of the group as a whole.

Social and Emotional Skills Supported

Attachment and Initiative

Materials Needed

hand soap

large bowls

butcher paper, about 3'

paint brushes

paper towels

tempera paint

Social & Emotional Lenses

Consider making an extra set of handprints and footprints on a paper to send home to each child's family. These tiny hands and feet continue to grow, and families will cherish these memories for years to come!

What to Do

▸ Explain to the children that together they will make a flag that represents their classroom, using their footprints and handprints.

▸ Show the children an American flag and other examples of other flags, explaining what the colors and symbols on the flag indicate.

▸ Ask the children what colors they would like their flag to be, and if they'd like to include any pictures or symbols.

▸ Next, lay the butcher paper in a wide-open area or outdoors.

▸ Prepare a bucket/bowl of warm, soapy water for rinsing feet when you are done. Have towels nearby as well.

▸ To make the footprints, have the children remove their socks and shoes. Paint the bottom of their feet with their choice of tempera paint. Have the children stand on the butcher paper to make their footprints.

▸ Once every child has made footprints, place the flag aside to dry. Plan to add the handprints in the same manner either later in the day, or on another day.

▸ Allow the children to express their creativity in designing the flag.

Our Family Flag

Try this activity at home to reinforce what your child learned about being part of a larger community.

What Your Child Will Learn

Your child needs to understand that she is part of a larger community. As you work together on a collaborative task such as this, there are many opportunities to talk about how your hands and feet can come together to do good things! Talk about volunteering, serving, and helping others in need, and even working together to clean up! Your child's social and emotional skills will continue to thrive as you help celebrate each individual, while also focusing on the strength of the group as a whole.

Materials Needed

hand soap	paint brushes
large bowls	paper towels
large piece of butcher paper	tempera paint

What to Do

▶ Explain to your child that together you will make a flag that represents your family, using your footprints and handprints.

▶ Show the child an American flag and examples of other flags, explaining what the colors and symbols on the flag indicate.

▶ Ask your child what colors he would like the flag to be, and if he would like to include any pictures or symbols.

▶ Once your child has decided on the colors, pictures, and symbols, you are ready to begin. Prepare a bucket/bowl of warm, soapy water. Have a towel nearby. Lay the butcher paper in an open area or outdoors.

▶ To make the footprints, have your child remove his socks and shoes. Paint the bottom of his feet with his choice of tempera paint. Have your child stand on the butcher paper to make his footprints. Repeat the procedure for your child's handprints, encouraging him to place his handprints wherever he desires.

▶ Encourage your child to express his creativity in designing the flag.

▶ Invite all family members to add their feet and hands as well, if possible!

*You can download this activity and the other at-home activities in this book at
www.centerforresilientchildren.org/SSES.

Still as Statues

Offers physical activities that use large muscles and expend energy.

What Children Will Learn

Children learn to move their bodies, slow down their bodies, and finally rest their bodies—all to the rhythm of the music. The more self-awareness a child can gain, the better he or she will be able to recognize states of excitement or even agitation in the body and find positive ways to release energy and calm down.

Social and Emotional Skills Supported

Initiative and Self-Control

Materials Needed

recorded music or a rhythm instrument

What to Do

▸ Introduce this experience by talking with the children about what a statue is.

▸ Show the children pictures and real-life examples of statues. Ask the children to imitate what they see in the picture or example.

▸ Explain that you are going to play a game in which they will move around the room to the music. When the music stops, they will "freeze" and become statues.

▸ Have someone start the music or play a simple rhythm on an instrument. When the music stops, everyone must become a "statue." Restart the music, and all statues can come alive!

▸ Offer specific encouragement: "Wow, Monet, your eyes are closed, and you're standing perfectly still."

▸ Play this game often. The expressive, free movement and stop-action develops children's body control and awareness, which promotes self-control.

▸ When the children are familiar with how to play the game, let them take turns stopping and starting the music.

▸ Because this activity can be lively, it is best to conclude it with calming music to help everyone settle down.

Social & Emotional Lenses
Self-control is a key protective factor and social and emotional skill that children need to be successful in school and in life! Learn more about protective factors at www.devereuxearly childhood.org

Still as Statues

Try this activity at home to reinforce what your child learned about self-regulation and self-awareness.

What Your Child Will Learn

Music is an excellent resource to help children develop self-regulation and self-control. Children learn to move their bodies, slow down their bodies, and finally rest their bodies—all to the rhythm of the music. The more self-awareness a child can gain, the better she will be able to recognize states of excitement or even agitation in her own body and find positive ways to release her energy and calm down.

Materials Needed

recorded music or a rhythm instrument

What to Do

▶ Talk to your child about what a statue is.

▶ Tell your child that you're going to play a game in which she will move around the room to the music. When the music stops, she will "freeze" and become a statue.

▶ Start the music or play a simple rhythm on an instrument. When the music stops, your child must become a "statue." Restart the music, encouraging the statue to come alive!!

▶ Offer acknowledgment: "Wow! Your eyes are closed, and you're standing very still."

▶ Play this game often. The expressive, free movement and stop-action develops your child's body control and awareness, which promotes self-control.

▶ Because this activity can be lively, it is best to conclude it with calming music to help your child settle down.

*You can download this activity and the other at-home activities in this book at www.centerforresilientchildren.org/SSES.

Everyone's Pet

Provide many opportunities for children to build language skills by talking with children and asking them open-ended questions throughout the day.

What Children Will Learn

Children gain a better understanding of responsibility when they take care of a pet (real or pretend). Realizing what is involved in remembering to feed, play with, and care for the pet will help the child learn independence and also understand the importance of helping others.

Social and Emotional Skills Supported

Attachment, Initiative, and Self-Control

Materials Needed

stuffed animal of your choice
journal (optional)

What to Do

▶ Select a stuffed animal to be "everyone's pet." Each child will get a chance to care for the pet. Make a schedule to send the pet home with each child over a weekend.

▶ Encourage the children (and their families) to take care of the pet as if it were real and to take pictures of the places they go with the pet. Have an adult write up the child's experiences with the pet to share with everyone else.

▶ When the child's turn with the pet is over, ask open-ended questions about the places the pet went, the foods it "ate," how well the pet "slept," and so on. One goal of this activity is to develop children's language skills, so encourage the children to ask questions of each other, as well.

▶ Help children begin to learn about helping take care of something or someone special!

▶ Children can also draw pictures or write about their experiences with the pet. Compile a class journal, and after every child has added to the journal, laminate it and put it in your reading area. **NOTE:** Take the stuffed animal home and wash it between visits to ensure it is clean and ready for the next trip. Depending on your program or classroom's preference and allergies of children, consider using a "non-stuffed" animal.

Social & Emotional Lenses
Did you have a pet when you were a child? If so, share your personal experiences with the children. What did you learn about owning a pet?

Everyone's Pet

Our class "pet" will be sent home with your child at some point during the school year.

What Your Child Will Learn

Children gain a better understanding of responsibility when they take care of a pet (real or pretend). Realizing what is involved in remembering to feed, play with, and care for the pet will help the child learn independence and also understand the importance of helping others. Having a group journal of the pet's experiences is a fun way to reflect on the many different adventures everyone got to enjoy with a special, shared friend.

Materials Needed

stuffed animal (sent home by your child's teacher)

group journal (sent home by your child's teacher)

What to Do

▶ Encourage your child to take care of the pet as if it were real and to take pictures of the places he goes with the pet.

▶ Talk with your child about the places the pet went, the foods it "ate," how well the pet "slept," and so on. Be sure to ask open-ended questions to develop your child's language skills.

▶ Help your child write about his experiences or draw pictures in the journal.

*You can download this activity and the other at-home activities in this book at
www.centerforresilientchildren.org/SSES.

Promoting Resilience Through Activities and Experiences

93

Promoting Resilience Through Daily Routines and Transitions

Having a predictable, yet flexible daily routine for children can help promote resilience. By carefully planning and organizing your day, you can avoid difficult transitions that may cause children to resist or act out. Children may become frustrated when they have to end an activity without warning or when they feel rushed through what they are doing. When you plan transitions thoughtfully, you may find that children respond and behave in more positive ways.

What Time Is It, Anyway?

Young children don't understand ideas about time—yesterday, today, tomorrow, hours, and minutes—in the same way that adults do. Providing children with clear and predictable routines and schedules helps them to feel secure and begin to understand the concepts of time. While they may not understand, "We will be going outside in an hour," they can understand, "We will be going outside after we have lunch."

What Research Says

When teachers and caregivers of preschool-aged children do not plan adequately in the daily schedule for transition times, behavioral issues can ensue. For example, if children are expected to wait long periods of time for others to finish activities or for a bus to arrive, children can have stressful and frustrating experiences, and often need to be reprimanded multiple times for touching things on the wall, poking their peers, talking, or squirming (Ratcliff, 2001).

All early childhood programs benefit from a regular activity schedule. When there is a written plan of daily activities, staff and families have a common understanding and ability to compare the program's actual performance with the stated intent (National Health and Safety Performance Standards, Second Edition, 2002).

Educators who spend time early in the year establishing clear procedures and routines have children who become more involved in academic tasks later on (Bohn, Roehrig, & Pressley, 2004).

In your efforts to promote children's social and emotional health and resilience, it is also important to be flexible and respond to the needs of the individual children. Sticking to a routine does not mean that you need to time things to the second. A successful routine allows for flexibility. Try to keep to your daily routine, but if there are any changes, make every attempt to explain this change to the children before the change occurs. Also, try not to make too many changes at once. When children have too many unknowns, they may appear anxious and start reacting negatively to the inconsistency.

What's Ahead

In this chapter you will find everyday strategies that can be used to support resilience through daily routines. Three key social and emotional skills that will be highlighted are: initiative, attachment, and self-control.

When you use strategies that focus on predictable daily routines, you support:

- ▶ Children's **initiative**. When daily routines are organized and take into consideration both individual and group needs, children are more inclined to take risks and explore their environment. Children are also better able to make choices and decisions when they have a daily schedule they can depend on.
- ▶ Children's **attachment**. Children feel safe and secure when adults provide predictable, yet flexible daily routines. This safety and trust helps build children's attachment to those in their environment.
- ▶ Children's **self-control**. Predictable routines help children learn to know what to expect. This sense of expectation helps them to learn to self-regulate.

10 Ways to Promote Resilience Using Daily Routines and Transitions

1. Establish and maintain a predictable schedule and consistent daily routines.

2. Help children learn to be flexible when circumstances arise that will alter the regular routine of the day.

3. Provide time in the daily schedule to expend energy and time to relax.

4. Plan for opportunities for indoor and outdoor play experiences.

5. Plan time in each day for imagination and dramatic play opportunities.

6. Plan enough time for routines so that children do not feel rushed.

7. Be organized, and help children prepare for transitions between events.

8. Involve children in carrying out routines and transitions.

9. Help children cope with separation times and reunions with caring adults.

10. Include supplies for personal care and cleanup, and teach children how to take care of themselves and their environment.

Clothespin Pictorial Schedule

Helps establish and maintain a predictable schedule and consistent daily routines.

What Children Will Learn

Going over the children's daily events and routines encourages them to be optimistic and to look forward to what's coming ahead. Children feel more secure, in control, and competent when they are aware of what will take place throughout their day. The ability to talk about and plan for the future is a skill we want children to possess as they grow, learn, and mature.

Social and Emotional Skills Supported

Attachment, Initiative, and Self-Control

Materials Needed

card stock or construction paper

clothespins

photos of the children carrying out daily classroom routines (putting their coats away, bringing art supplies to the table, cleaning up, and so on)

ribbon or string

scissors

tape or glue

What to Do

▶ Take pictures of the children carrying out daily routines.

▶ Mount each photo onto a piece of heavy construction paper or card stock. Laminate or cover the photos with clear contact paper.

▶ Hang a piece of string or ribbon (approximately two feet long) low across a wall so children can see it and reach it.

▶ Talk about the order of the day's events and routines with the children, allowing them to use the clothespins to attach the corresponding photos to the ribbon or string, in order.

▶ Continue with each photo until you have outlined the children's entire day.

▶ Make every attempt to do this each day as an excellent way to establish and maintain a predictable and consistent schedule and routine.

Social & Emotional Lenses

Do you like knowing what your day will bring? We all feel more safe and secure when we know what is coming next!

Clothespin Pictorial Schedule

Try this activity at home to reinforce your child's understanding of her schedule and routine.

What Your Child Will Learn

Your child feels more secure, in control, and competent when she is aware of what will take place throughout the day. The ability to talk about and plan for the future is a skill your child should possess as she grows, learns, and matures.

Materials Needed

card stock or construction paper

clothespins

photos of your child carrying out daily routines (brushing her teeth, watching TV, resting, bathing, having a meal, and so on)

ribbon or string

scissors

tape or glue

What to Do

▶ Take pictures of your child carrying out daily routines.

▶ Using the photos you have taken, mount each onto a heavy piece of construction paper or cardstock. It's a good idea to laminate or cover the photos with clear contact paper.

▶ Hang a piece of string or ribbon (approximately two feet long) low across a wall where your child can readily see and reach it.

▶ As each day begins, go over the order of the day's events and routines with your child.

▶ Show your child how to use the clothespins to attach a photo to the ribbon or string.

▶ Continue with each photo until you have outlined your child's entire day.

▶ Make every attempt to do this each day as an excellent way to establish and maintain a predictable and consistent schedule and routine.

NOTE: Creating any type of consistent schedule for your child will be helpful. Simply drawing a few pictures on a white board or piece of paper showing "breakfast, school, nana's house, home for dinner, bedtime" might be all your child needs to feel secure about her daily schedule. Whether you create a picture schedule for home, it is important to review your child's daily schedule with her regularly, to help her have a sense of a consistent routine.

A Star Marks the Spot

Helps children learn to be flexible when circumstances arise that will alter the regular routine of the day.

What Children Will Learn

Change can be good when it is shared with the child *before* the circumstance arrives. Children learn to adjust and adapt to change when adults make every effort to help them understand when and how the regular routine of the day may be altered.

Social and Emotional Skills Supported

Attachment, Initiative, and Self-Control

Materials Needed

large star cut from construction paper
pictorial schedule (see Clothespin Pictorial Schedule on page 98), or a
    whiteboard with a simple schedule written or drawn

What to Do

▶ Think about any changes there may be in the children's schedule for the day.

▶ To make the children aware of the change, place a star on or near that part of the day in their pictorial schedule. (If using a whiteboard, put the star near the new activity or the change.) If possible, allow one of the children to put the star in the spot for the new activity, and possibly even help you present what the change will be.

▶ Show the children where you have placed the star. Explain the change and tell them what will happen as a result.

▶ Allow the children to ask questions and talk about any confusion or anxiety there might be about the change in schedule.

Social & Emotional Lenses
Change is difficult for everyone. Children and adults who are more resilient can adjust more smoothly to changes and "go with the flow" more easily.

A Star Marks the Spot

Try this activity at home to reinforce what your child learned about the importance of being flexible when plans change.

What Your Child Will Learn

Change can be good when it is shared with the child *before* the circumstance arrives. Children learn to adjust and adapt to change when adults make every effort to help them understand when and how the regular routine of the day may be altered.

Materials Needed

large star cut from construction paper

pictorial schedule (see outline below), or a whiteboard with a simple schedule written or drawn

What to Do

▶ If you do not have a pictorial or written daily schedule for your child, try these simple steps to create one:

◀ Take pictures of your child carrying out everyday daily routines.

◀ Mount photos onto a heavy piece of construction paper or card stock.

◀ Hang a piece of string or ribbon (approximately two feet long) low across a wall where your child can readily see and reach it.

◀ Add the photos in order to make up your child's daily schedule.

◀ At the start of each day, go over the day's events and routines with your child.

◀ Make every attempt to do this each day as an excellent way to establish and maintain a predictable and consistent schedule and routine.

▶ If you already have a pictorial or written daily schedule for your child, proceed to the steps below.

▶ Take a moment to think about any changes there may be in your child's schedule for the day.

▶ To make your child aware of the change, place a star on or near that part of the day in the pictorial schedule. (If using a whiteboard, put the star near the new activity or the change.)

▶ Show your child where you have placed the star. Explain the change and what will happen as a result.

*You can download this activity and the other at-home activities in this book at www.centerforresilientchildren.org/SSES.

On the Dance Floor

Provides a way to expend energy and a way to relax.

What Children Will Learn

Music and movement are great ways for children to express themselves. This activity allows the children to begin to regulate their bodies into states of relaxation and states of excitement. When children can become more aware of these contrasting states of high and low energy, they gain more self-control.

Social and Emotional Skills Supported

Attachment, Initiative, and Self-Control

Materials Needed

music
music player

What to Do

▸ Invite the children to join you in a large, open space and explain that you are going to play a song. As long as the music is playing, they should dance! As soon as the music stops, you will shout out a command that they must follow.

▸ When you first stop the music, shout "elbow-to-elbow." Elbow-to-elbow means the children must find a partner and freeze, touching only the elbow of their partner. **NOTE:** Be sure to emphasize being "gentle" in our touches with others, to ensure the activity stays fun and safe for all.

▸ Offer acknowledgment and encouragement for the children's effort: "Julia, you are trying so hard to hold your knee in the air!"

▸ Continue to play the music. When the music stops, shout "hand-to-hand." Hand-to-hand means the children must find a partner and freeze, touching only the hand of their partner.

▸ Continue to stop and go as long as the children seem involved. The following are a few other commands you can use:
   ◂ heel-to-heel
   ◂ head-to-head
   ◂ knee-to-knee
   ◂ ear-to-ear

Social & Emotional Lenses
Take time to dance, exercise, and move your own body to stay healthy and happy.

Use this activity at home to provide your child with an opportunity to expend energy.

Materials Needed

music

music player

What to Do

▸ Invite your child to join you in a large, open space and explain that when she hears music, she should dance. As soon as the music stops, she should "freeze," and stay in that position until the music starts up again.

▸ Acknowledge and encourage your child's effort: "Julia, you are trying so hard to hold your knee in the air!" Be silly and encourage your child to have a good time!

*You can download this activity and the other at-home activities in this book at
www.centerforresilientchildren.org/SSES.

It's My Choice!

Ensures that you plan time in the daily schedule for indoor and outdoor play experiences.

What Children Will Learn

The great thing about these activities is they can be carried out both indoors and out. Giving children choices helps them feel in control. As children mature, the confidence that they gain as they make choices will support them on their road to resilience.

Social and Emotional Skills Supported

Attachment, Initiative, and Self-Control

Materials Needed

beach ball (or cotton balls or Ping-Pong balls)

blanket (or beach towel)

hula-hoops®

large sheet of clear plastic (big enough to have several children working on it at one time) available in your local fabric or craft store

music

paintbrushes

tempera paint

What to Do

▸ Present the following choices to children and let them decide what they would like to do.

See-Through Art

▸ Invite the children who are interested to join you in creating a group mural.

▸ Attach the plastic to a fence or other surface where children can work at their eye-level.

▸ Encourage the children to paint and decorate the plastic. When you're finished, the mural will be a beautiful and meaningful addition to your classroom.

Blanket Ball

▸ Ask the children to hold the edges of a blanket. Put a beach ball in the middle and have them toss it in the air. How high can they make it go? How far can they toss it?

▸ With smaller groups, or just two children, try using a large beach towel and cotton balls or Ping-Pong balls.

Mirror Partners

▸ Have the children find a partner or have an adult pair up with a child.

▸ One child moves a body part (for example, leg, arm, foot, and so on). The other child copies her partner's movements.

▸ Encourage the children to switch roles.

Musical Hula-Hoops®

▸ Lay the hoops on the ground and start the music. Tell the children to move until the music stops! Once the music stops, the children must get inside a hoop.

▸ Tell the children to stand up and take away one hoop. Restart the music, and repeat until all the hoops are gone.

▸ Encourage and applaud the children who cooperate and make room in the hoops for their classmates.

Social & Emotional Lenses
Even when it's gloomy and the weather isn't great, these fun activities will help children cooperate!

Set up these activities at home, and invite your child to choose which one to do.

What Your Child Will Learn

The great thing about these activities is they can be carried out both indoors and out. Giving children choices helps them feel in control. As children mature, the confidence that they gain as they make choices will support them on their road to resilience.

Materials Needed

beach ball (or cotton balls)

blanket (or beach towel)

large sheet of clear plastic (available in
    your local fabric or craft store)

paintbrushes

tempera paint

What to Do

▶ The following activities are examples of things you can do with your child. Allow your child to choose which activity she wants to do.

See-Through Art

▶ Create a mural with your child.

▶ Attach plastic to a fence or other surface where your child can work at her eye level.

▶ Encourage your child to paint and decorate the plastic. When she is finished, the mural will be a beautiful and meaningful addition to your home.

Blanket Ball

▶ Have your child hold one end of a blanket (or beach towel) and you hold the other. Put a beach ball (or cotton balls) in the middle and toss them in the air. How high can you make them go? How far can you toss them?

Mirror Partners

▶ Stand facing your child.

▶ Have your child move a body part (leg, arm, foot, or other part) and you copy the movement.

▶ Switch roles. Have fun!

Musical Hula-Hoops®

▶ Lay the hoops on the ground and start the music. Tell the children to move until the music stops! Once the music stops, the children must get inside a hoop.

▶ Tell the children to stand up and take away one hoop. Restart the music, and repeat until all the hoops are gone.

▶ Encourage and applaud the children who cooperate and make room in the hoops for their classmates.

*You can download this activity and the other at-home activities in this book at
www.centerforresilientchildren.org/SSES.

Let's Pretend Charades

Provide time in each day for imagination and dramatic play opportunities.

What Children Will Learn

The ability to be imaginative and expressive directly relates to resilience. Continue to encourage children's creative expression. In a time when so much of our children's play has become computer-directed or packaged, we must revisit those days of simple pretend-play. After all, this is where children's dreams and hopes for tomorrow are created.

Social and Emotional Skills Supported

Attachment, Initiative, and Self-Control

Materials Needed

photos or drawn pictures of dramatic play roles that the children will be able to act out (Select pictures that will be easy for the children to act out, such as a baseball player, ballerina, rock star, doctor, teacher, bird, or rabbit.)

What to Do

▶ Collect a number of photographs, pictures from magazines, or free clip art from the Internet before this activity.
▶ Tell the children you are going to play a game of pretend.
▶ Call one child up front for her turn. Show the child a picture and tell her to try to act out the picture without using any words.
▶ Involve the other children in a guessing game about who or what the child is pretending to be.
▶ Providing props and other materials will help make the experience more creative and imaginative.
▶ As always, adults are encouraged to join in the dramatic fun!

Social & Emotional Lenses
Many of the interactive games of former generations, such as Ring Around the Rosie, I Spy, London Bridge, and Follow the Leader, are worth introducing to the children of this generation… interactive, cooperative, creative games boost brain-power—plus, they are FUN!

Let's Pretend Charades

Try this activity at home to reinforce what your child learned about expressing herself.

What Your Child Will Learn

The ability to be imaginative and expressive directly relates to resilience. Continue to encourage your child's creative expression. In a time when so much of children's play has become computer-directed or packaged, we must revisit those days of simple pretend-play. After all, this is where children's dreams and hopes for tomorrow are created.

Materials Needed

photos or drawn pictures of dramatic play roles your child will be able to act out (Select pictures that will be easy for your child to act out, such as a baseball player, ballerina, rock star, doctor, teacher, bird, or rabbit.)

What to Do

▶ Collect photographs, pictures from magazines, or free clip art from the Internet before this activity.
▶ Introduce this activity by having your child sit near you. Explain that you are going to play a game of pretend.
▶ Show your child a picture.
▶ Encourage your child to act out the picture; for example, if the picture is a rabbit, your child may hop around.
▶ Providing props and other materials will help make the experience more creative and imaginative.
▶ As always, you should join in the dramatic fun!

*You can download this activity and the other at-home activities in this book at
www.centerforresilientchildren.org/SSES.

108   SOCIALLY STRONG, EMOTIONALLY SECURE

Leave a Little Wiggle Room

Plan enough time for routines so that children do not feel rushed.

What Children Will Learn

Providing a little wiggle room helps everyone stay calm and in control of their emotions. It also sets the stage for opportunities for success. When rushed, children may not be able to successfully finish a task or activity. They often will grow frustrated and may even give up. When adults provide children with a little wiggle room, children learn that they can be successful in their attempts to do things on their own.

Social and Emotional Skills Supported

Attachment, Initiative, and Self-Control

Materials Needed

Special Note: The better your observation practices, the better you get to know the children in your care. You will be able to see their strengths and needs when you follow these guidelines for conducting and recording running record observations.

What to Do

▶ Spend some time observing the children and notice those times in the day when they experience feelings of rush and haste. For example, maybe you have noticed that it takes the children a long time to put on their coats or to clean up.

▶ Using what you have learned from observing the children, build in extra time for the children to carry out those routines without feeling rushed. For example, if the children struggle to get ready to go outside, allow more time for this transition.

▶ At times, you may find that you are allowing the children too much time for a transition or routine, and you notice that children begin to behave in ways that challenge you. In these cases, find ways to make the time spent in that routine more appropriate for the children's needs.

Are your observations...

▶ **Accurate?** Do you observe each child in a variety of settings such as: active and quiet activities, child-initiated and adult-directed activities, various times of day and days of the week, and in a variety of play situations from solo play to small-group to large-group play? To get an accurate picture, you must conduct observations across many situations and settings.

▶ **Objective?** Do you record just what you see and just what you hear? Recording only the facts in an objective manner gives a clear picture of what happened.

▶ **Complete?** Do you include the beginning, middle, and end of a play scenario in order to see the complete picture? Capturing antecedents (those events or factors that might have caused a behavior), behaviors, and consequences of both positive and more challenging interactions will help paint a complete picture of the child's skills.

Social & Emotional Lenses
Observation is one of the best tools that teachers and families have to get to know each child's strengths and needs.

Leave a Little Wiggle Room

Try doing this at home to help your child feel less rushed and to give him more of an opportunity to succeed in a task.

Materials Needed

What to Do

▶ Spend some time observing your child and take note of those times in the day when he is experiencing feelings of rush and haste. For example, maybe you have noticed that it takes your child a great deal of time to put on his coat or clean up.

▶ Allow your child extra time when carrying out a routine that often feels rushed or hurried. For example, if getting ready to go outside frustrates him, give him more time to get ready. This will help him to feel the sense of accomplishment that comes with accomplishing tasks without feeling rushed.

▶ At times, you may find that you are allowing your child too much time for a transition or routine, and he may begin to act out in ways that are challenging to you. In these cases, find ways to make the time spent in that routine more appropriate for your child's needs.

*You can download this activity and the other at-home activities in this book at www.centerforresilientchildren.org/SSES.

It's Almost Time!

Helps you become organized in order to help children prepare for transitions between events.

What Children Will Learn

As adults, we understand how time can "get away from us." The same is true for children. When using a clock and visual cues, adults help children learn to organize the time they spend playing and learning. Children will feel much less "hurried" when they can see the time to finish an activity is slowly approaching.

Social and Emotional Skills Supported

Attachment, Initiative, and Self-Control

Materials Needed

large (plastic) clock
small removable stickers

What to Do

▶ Place a clock (preferably one made from plastic) low enough for the children to see.

▶ Explain to the children that you will use this clock to help them know when it may be time to start or stop an activity.

▶ Talk with the children about the clock. Point out the "long hand" and the "short hand."

▶ Use the stickers to mark the time you would like the children to be prepared for a transition or event. For example, if the children have only 15 minutes to play and the current time is 11:15, place a sticker by the number six on the clock and let the children know that when the "long" minute hand starts to point at the sticker, it will be time to clean up!

▶ When the time has come and gone, remove the sticker. When you want to prepare children for the next transition, you can use a new sticker.

Social & Emotional Lenses
Everyone, adults and children alike, appreciates having an idea of when they will need to move on to the next event or activity!

It's Almost Time!

Try this at home to help your child prepare for transitions.

What Your Child Will Learn

As adults, we understand how time can "get away from us." The same is true for children. When using a clock and visual cues, you can help your child learn to organize the time she spends playing and learning. Your child will feel much less "hurried" when she can see the time to finish an activity is slowly approaching.

Materials Needed

large (plastic) clock
small removable stickers

What to Do

▸ Place a clock (preferably one made from plastic) low enough for your child to see.

▸ Explain to your child that you will use this clock to help her know when it may be time to start or stop an activity.

▸ Talk with your child about the clock. Point out in particular the "long hand" and the "short hand."

▸ Use the stickers to mark the time you would like your child to be prepared for a transition or event. For example, if your child has 15 minutes to play and the current time is 11:15, place a sticker by the number six on the clock and let your child know that when the "long" minute hand starts to point at the sticker, it will be time to clean up!

▸ When the time has come and gone, remove the sticker. When you want to prepare your child for another transition, you can use a new sticker.

*You can download this activity and the other at-home activities in this book at
www.centerforresilientchildren.org/SSES.

Together We're Better

Involves children in carrying out routines and transitions.

What Children Will Learn

Whenever possible throughout the day, make every attempt to involve the children in carrying out routines and transitions. The children can set up the chairs for story time or they can wipe the table after lunch. When you allow the children to help carry out routines and transitions, an internal sense of pride and accomplishment takes place within them that helps them smile on the inside!

Social and Emotional Skills Supported

Attachment, Initiative, and Self-Control

Materials Needed

napkins

plates and cups

utensils

What to Do

▸ Show the children how to set the table properly for a meal. You may wish to draw an example on paper using markers or crayons.

▸ At meal time, ask the children to set the table for the class.

▸ Offer verbal acknowledgment and encouragement. Thank the children for their effort: "Jarrod, you walked slowly and were concentrating really hard as you carried that cup across the room!"

▸ Look for other ways that the children can help carry out routines and transitions.

Social & Emotional Lenses
Children love to help adults. Let children help you whenever possible, and everyone will smile!

Try this activity at home to give your child the opportunity to be involved in a routine.

What Your Child Will Learn

Whenever possible throughout the day, make every attempt to involve your child in carrying out routines and transitions. Your child can set the table for dinner, help with laundry, and so on. When you invite your child to help carry out routines and transitions, she feels an internal sense of pride and accomplishment that makes her smile on the inside!

Materials Needed

anything required to carry out a routine of your choice (see below)

What to Do

▶ Choose a routine to demonstrate for your child.

▶ You might choose "how to set or clear the table," "how to wash or dry the dishes," "how to feed the pet," "how to make a bed," "how to sort laundry into colors or fold the laundry," or any other routine you do in your home.

▶ After you demonstrate, let your child practice. As you work together to help your child learn this routine, talk about how we can learn from and help each other.

▶ Offer verbal acknowledgment and encouragement. Thank your child for her effort: "Jane, you were concentrating really hard as you folded that shirt."

▶ Think of other ways that your child can help with routines and include her in those activities.

*You can download this activity and the other at-home activities in this book at www.centerforresilientchildren.org/SSES.

Promoting Resilience Through Daily Routines and Transitions

115

Something to Talk About

Helps children cope with separation times and reunions with caring adults.

What Children Will Learn

Separating from loved ones is not easy. Often, transitioning from one environment to the next is difficult for children. Helping bridge that transition is important, and this activity might be perfect for some of the children in your setting who struggle with separations and reunions.

Social and Emotional Skill Supported

Attachment

Materials Needed

notebook, index cards, or other way of passing on a short note between home and school, and vice versa

What to Do

▶ You do not need to perform this activity with every child, every day. Some children need more support with this transition than others.

▶ Explain to the child's family members that you have an idea to help ease your child into their school day, and also, ease them back into the families' care at the end of the school day.

▶ Tell them that you will write down in a notebook or on an index card one special moment the child had during the day to share with them. It could be something the child enjoyed doing, the name of a friend she played with and what they did together, or something the child shared with others at group time or another time during the day.

▶ Family members can use the information to help spark discussion with their child and ease the transition from school back to home. When the child is ready to go home at the end of the day, the family can read this personal message from school and have something specific to talk about right away, which might help ease the transition from school back to home.

▶ Suggest to families that they might do the same thing—writing one thing the child did that morning or the night before in a notebook or on an index card. When the child returns to school the next day, the teachers will have something to ask the child about that will help the child ease into the transition from home back to school.

▶ The child will feel special, and know that the adults in her life are communicating about what she likes and does. In addition, having something to talk about immediately will help the child feel noticed and loved.

Social & Emotional Lenses
Take some time to reflect on your important relationships. What ways are you working to maintain and nurture connections with these special individuals?

Help your child make the transition between home and school, and then from school back to home. These transitions are often not easy for children, and this activity might help make things go more smoothly. Having one specific occurrence to talk about right away with your child might help get the conversation going!

What Your Child Will Learn

Separating from loved ones is not easy for children (or family members). Often, transitioning from one environment to the next is difficult for children. Helping bridge that transition is important, and this activity might be perfect for your child if she struggles with separations and reunions.

Materials Needed

notebook, index cards, or other way of passing notes between home and school

What to Do

▶ Each day, try to write one thing in this notebook or on an index card about something special your child recently did or said when she was with you.

▶ At home, you could write about something your child really enjoyed doing the night before or that morning before school, the name of a friend or relative she recently played with, something your child shared with another person, a special meal your child enjoyed, a comment your child said or a cute thing she did, or anything that was a special moment for your child.

▶ When your child gets to school in the morning, I will read this message from home and have something personal to talk about right away with your child that might help ease that transition into the school day.

▶ At school, I will do the same thing! I will note one thing your child did at school during the day and write it in the notebook or on an index card. When you arrive to pick up your child, or, when your child arrives back home, you will have something specific to ask your child about that will help her ease into the transition from school back to home. Your child will feel special, and know that the adults in her life are communicating about what she likes and does. In addition, having something special to talk about immediately will help your child feel noticed and loved.

*You can download this activity and the other at-home activities in this book at www.centerforresilientchildren.org/SSES.

A Season for Cleaning

Encourages children to take care of themselves and their environment.

What Children Will Learn

Involving children in the care and maintenance of their environment helps them feel part of a community. With this sense of connectedness, the children feel safe to learn and grow. By keeping appropriate cleaning items nearby, children learn that they play a role in keeping the environment clean, both indoors and out.

Social and Emotional Skills Supported

Attachment and Initiative

Materials Needed

aprons (optional)

child-sized brooms, mops, feather dusters

poster board or a white board

spray bottles with water

What to Do

▶ Talk with the children about how important it is to keep our environment and favorite places to play and learn clean and well cared for.

▶ With the children, create a master checklist on a board or large piece of paper that lists everything you plan to clean. Use photos of the things you plan to clean in addition to the words if the children are pre- or early readers.

▶ Provide the children with the cleaning item(s) they will be working with (brooms, mops, feather dusters, and so on).

▶ Let the children clean/dust chairs, tables, and bookshelves. Support and join in with the children as they work. Offer lots of physical acknowledgment and verbal encouragement for their efforts (pats on the back, thumbs up sign, smiles, "We're all working together and this place is looking clean!").

▶ With the children, revisit your master cleaning list, and check off the completed items.

▶ Applaud the children for their effort and teamwork. Let them know these same cleaning items are available anytime they want to use them—really, *anytime*!

Social & Emotional Lenses

Even young children can participate in keeping their world safe and clean. It is never too early to start to share the message of how to take care of the places we play, work, learn, and live!

A Season for Cleaning

Try this activity at home to reinforce what your child learned about taking care of herself and her environment.

What Your Child Will Learn

Involving your child in the care and maintenance of her environment helps her feel part of the family and part of a community. With this sense of connectedness, your child feels safe to learn and grow. By keeping appropriate cleaning items nearby, your child learns that she plays a role in keeping the environment clean, both indoors and out.

Materials Needed

apron (optional)

child-sized brooms, mops, feather dusters

spray bottles with water

What to Do

- Explain to your child that it is "a season for cleaning." Create a master checklist together of everything you plan to clean.
- Provide your child with the cleaning item(s) she will be working with (brooms, mops, feather dusters, and so on).
- Let your child clean/dust chairs, tables, and bookshelves. Support and join in with your child as she works and learns. Offer lots of physical acknowledgment and verbal encouragement for her efforts (pats on the back, thumbs-up sign, smiles, "We're working together and this place is looking clean!", and so on).
- With your child, revisit your master cleaning list, and check off the completed items.
- Applaud your child for her effort and teamwork.
- As an ongoing way to help involve your child or children in keeping your home tidy, assign a few small jobs, such as helping to set or clear the table, organizing toys into the right areas, making her bed, helping feed a pet, and so on.
- Set up a system to remind everyone about the ways they can help, such as a chart or checklist.

*You can download this activity and the other at-home activities in this book at www.centerforresilientchildren.org/SSES.

Promoting Resilience Through the Play and Learning Environment

Have you ever found yourself relaxing by a running stream or enjoying the splendor of watching an early morning sunrise? Or have you ever found yourself tensing up as soon as you enter a bright, crowded grocery or department store? Our environment can affect our mood, how we interact with others, our behavior, and even our resilience and ability to "bounce back."

Young children are also sensitive to their surrounding environment. Their behavior and their development are affected by how we arrange both our indoor and outdoor spaces. When designing classroom environments, it is important to take into consideration the likes, dislikes, and cultures of the children and families enrolled in the program. The same is true for the home environment. Well-designed spaces that allow for movement, active, imaginative, and quiet play contribute to children's overall development and well-being.

What Research Says

Adults play a central role in creating a warm and caring program environment that encourages both emotional and social learning. By establishing this supportive climate, teachers can help young children discover themselves and begin to establish positive relationships (Epstein, 2009).

Well-organized, well-equipped, and well-maintained environments support program quality by fostering the learning, comfort, health and safety of those who use the program. Program quality is enhanced by also creating a welcoming and accessible setting for children, families, and staff (Hyson, 2008).

Higher classroom quality has been linked with increases in expressive language skills (Mashburn et al., 2008), fewer behavioral problems (Burchinal, Peisner-Feinberg, Bryant & Clifford, 2000; Rimm-Kaufman, LaParo, Downer & Pianta, 2005); and higher behavioral engagement (Downer, Rimm-Kaufman & Pianta, 2005; Pianta et al., 2002).

Have a Goal

The best way to think about your environment is to think about how it can help you achieve your goals with children.

Goal 1: Our rooms should make children feel welcome and safe.

▸ Keep toys and materials clean, carefully stored, and not broken. This makes children feel that they too will be kept safe.

▸ Give children a place to keep their own belongings. This makes them feel welcome and included.

▸ Hang pictures of children's family members at eye level. This makes them feel more at home in the classroom.

▸ Hang pictures of children and adults from different ethnic groups and cultures, especially those represented in your program. This shows children that all people are welcome at your school.

▸ Keep books, pillows, clothes, and other home-like artifacts in the classroom. This gives children a message of respect and acceptance of different cultures.

Goal 2: Our rooms should encourage self-directed play and imagination.

▸ Keep toys and materials on low, open shelves that children can reach easily. This allows them to feel secure in finding what they want to use.

▸ Teach children to be creative and use their imaginations when they are faced with the challenge of not having enough materials and supplies. For example, a block can become a milk carton for their housekeeping play and a shoe can become a pretend telephone.

Goal 3: Our rooms should be arranged so that children can be away from others when needed.

▸ Provide a supervised place for children to go for privacy if they feel tired of interacting with their peers. Many children are in child care for 10 to 12 hours a day, and may occasionally need a break from other children.

What's Ahead

In this chapter you will find everyday strategies that can be used not only to promote resilience through the play and learning environment, but also to promote overall classroom quality. In the home environment, these strategies will help families create safe, meaningful spaces for children to grow, learn, and play. Three key social and emotional skills that will be highlighted are: initiative, attachment, and self-control.

When you use strategies that focus on play and learning, you support:

▸ Children's **initiative**. In high-quality environments, opportunities abound for children to exhibit their initiative. Children can reach materials, which encourages them to be autonomous. Shelves and learning center areas are clean, well organized and labeled, which helps children make choices about what and where they would like to play. In environments rich in quality, children explore special interests in depth, which increases their ability to pay attention and focus on a task—a skill they will need in school and life.

▸ Children's **attachment**. Children feel secure when they have a predictable, consistent environment where they can grow and explore. This safety allows relationships to grow—between adult and child as well as between the children themselves.

▸ Children's **self-control.** Well-organized spaces that reflect each child's interests, developmental level, and culture help support the skills of self-regulation and self-control. Learning to recognize and name feelings also takes place when items in the environment support this developing skill. Children gain self-control, learn to solve problems, and grow in confidence when they can explore and express their feelings and learn to play with others.

10 Ways to Promote Resilience Through the Play and Learning Environment

1. Provide toys and materials that reflect children's current skills and interests.

2. Provide children with safe spaces to play and explore.

3. Place toys and materials on low open shelves or containers within children's reach.

4. Provide children with a few be-by-myself spaces that are private but still visible to adults.

5. Provide storage and display areas to keep projects before and after they have been completed.

6. Create a friendly and welcoming atmosphere for all who enter.

7. Provide a range of open-ended materials, from simple to complex, that offer different levels of challenge.

8. Provide items that help children learn to explore and express their feelings and develop a sense of self.

9. Help children release energy throughout the day by providing materials, equipment, and space for indoor gross motor play.

10. Offer duplicates of favorite items, and consider rotating toys in and out of the play area to keep materials fresh and interesting.

Individual Theme Kits

Provides toys and materials that reflect children's current skills and interests.

What Children Will Learn

When adults take the time to learn about children's interests, and plan for activities and play experiences that encourage these interests, children learn that adults are caring, connected, and supportive. They will be more willing to cooperate, take an interest in what their friends enjoy, and explore their interests in more detail.

Social and Emotional Skills Supported

Initiative and Self-Control

Materials Needed

old/used plastic containers or shoe boxes
small items and materials related to anything that interests the children

What to Do

▶ Spend several days observing and listening to the children, asking them questions about the things that interest them. As you learn more about what they're interested in, begin collecting items related to those themes to create their theme kits. Kits can be created with individual children in mind but should be available for all to use. **NOTE:** It is not necessary to make a theme kit for every child!

▶ As you collect items representing a particular interest, place them in one of the containers. For example, if you have noticed that the children currently have an interest in dogs, you can collect plastic dogs, pictures of dogs, small books about dogs, and so on.

▶ Once you have enough materials in the container, let the children help label and decorate it and talk to them about all the wonderful items inside.

▶ Use theme kits to enhance the play experience anywhere inside or outside. Children can even take them to cots or mats during rest time.

Social & Emotional Lenses
Be sure the materials in the learning environment aren't just the "same ones you've always used." Set up interest areas that are reflective of and as unique as each new group of children!

Individual Theme Kits

Try this activity at home to show your child that you are interested in his interests!

What Your Child Will Learn

When you take the time to learn about your child's interests and plan for activities and play experiences that encourage these interests, your child learns that you are interested and tuned in to him. It sends a clear message to your child of caring, connection, and support. Your child will be able to explore his interests in more detail, allowing his imagination to soar.

Materials Needed

container (such as a shoebox)

small items and materials related to something your child is interested in

What to Do

▶ Spend several days observing and listening to your child, and ask him questions about the things that interest him.

▶ Collect items that represent those interests and place them in the container. For example, if you have noticed that your child has an interest in dogs, you can collect plastic dogs, pictures of dogs, small books about dogs, and so on.

▶ Once you have enough materials in the container, let your child help label and decorate it and talk to your child about all the wonderful items inside.

▶ Use the theme kit to enhance your child's play experience anywhere, even on family trips to visit relatives or friends.

*You can download this activity and the other at-home activities in this book at
www.centerforresilientchildren.org/SSES.

Walking on My Knees for You

Provides children with safe spaces to play and explore.

What Children Will Learn

By taking the time to walk on your knees through the children's world, you show the children that their perspective is important to you. By asking questions about what they like and would like to change about their learning spaces, you show the children that you care about their opinions and will try to use their input to make changes when possible.

Social and Emotional Skills Supported

Attachment, Initiative, and Self-Control

Materials Needed

What to Do

▶ Tell the children that you are going to pretend to be their size for a few minutes. Ask them to guide you around their play and learning spaces while you ask questions like:

"Can you reach everything you want?" (You can ask this, but sometimes the things they may want to touch are out of their reach for safety reasons.)

"Are there things at your eye level and within your reach that maybe should be for a teacher's or other adult's hands only?"

"What do you like about this space?"

"What would you like to change?"

▶ Keep in mind that some of the suggestions from the children may not be possible, but it is still nice to ask for their input as you figure out what adaptations might need to be made.

▶ Do a safety check, making sure to move out of reach anything that is a safety issue.

▶ Consider children's suggestions for things they would like to reach that they cannot. Could you safely move those items? Or, do they need to stay out of reach?

▶ After you walk through each of the spaces at the children's eye level, tell them what you saw and learned about where they play and learn. Discuss how fun it was to see their world at their level!

NOTE: Some teachers may not be able to walk on their knees, so, making sure that you look around from the child's perspective is the important focus of this activity.

Social & Emotional Lenses

Now that you have taken a look at the classroom from the children's point of view, what one thing can you change to better support the building of initiative, attachment or self-control?

Walking on My Knees for You

Try this activity at home to show your child that his perspective is important to you, and that you care about making his play area safe and secure.

What Your Child Will Learn
By taking the time to walk on your knees through your child's world, you show him that his perspective is important to you. By asking questions about what he likes and would like to change about his living spaces you show him that you care about his opinions.

Materials Needed
none

What to Do
NOTE: This activity is fun to try when you know a younger child or baby will be visiting your home. Involving your child in "baby-proofing" will help him feel responsible and prepared.

▶ Tell your child that you are going to pretend to be his size for a few minutes. Ask him to guide you around his play area while you ask questions like:

   "Can you reach everything you want?" (You can ask this, but sometimes the things he may want to touch are out of his reach for safety reasons.)

   "Are there things at your eye level and within your reach that maybe should be for a grownup's hands only?"

   "What do you like about this space?"

   "What would you like to change?"

▶ Keep in mind that some of the suggestions from your child may not be possible, but it is still nice to ask for his input as you figure out what adaptations might need to be made.

▶ Do a safety check, making sure to move anything potentially dangerous to a safer place.

▶ After you walk through your child's play space at his eye level, tell him what you saw and learned. Discuss how fun it was to see your child's world from this perspective!

*You can download this activity and the other at-home activities in this book at
www.centerforresilientchildren.org/SSES.

130   SOCIALLY STRONG, EMOTIONALLY SECURE

Where Does It Go?

Helps create a better environment by placing toys and materials on low open shelves or in containers within children's reach.

What Children Will Learn

Although it may not seem like it sometimes, children actually enjoy organization and a world that makes sense. Clutter and disorganization can confuse children about expectations and about their own safety and care. When we involve children in the clean-up process, we send the message that we care about their spaces, and we want them to care too. Storing toys and materials on low, open shelves also offers an open invitation for children to access what they need to be imaginative and playful.

Social and Emotional Skills Supported

Initiative and Self-Control

Materials Needed

bin/basket

toys and materials from low shelves around the classroom or home

What to Do

▶ Take a bin/basket and discreetly collect a few things from various low shelves in the classroom. Label it the "Where Does It Go?" bin.

▶ Present the children with the "Where Does it Go?" bin, and explain to them that you have all these lost toys and other items that can't find their homes.

▶ Invite the children to help these lost toys and materials find their homes. One at a time, take an object from your bin and ask for a child to help it find its home.

▶ This activity is a great way to introduce new toys and materials and a wonderful opportunity to practice picking up!

Social & Emotional Lenses
Think how clutter and disorganization can make you feel overwhelmed and out-of-control of your own life. Make a plan to start weeding through any clutter today!

Where Does It Go?

Try this activity at home to reinforce the importance of organization in your child's environment.

What Your Child Will Learn

Although it may not seem like it, sometimes children actually enjoy organization and a world that makes sense. Clutter and disorganization can confuse your child about expectations and about her own safety and care. When you involve your child in the clean-up process, you send the message that you care about her spaces, and you want her to care too. Storing toys and materials on low, open shelves offers an open invitation for your child to access what she needs to be imaginative and playful.

Materials Needed

bin/basket, toys and materials from low shelves around the house

What to Do

▶ Take a bin/basket and discreetly collect a few things from various low shelves in your child's play area. Label it the "Where Does It Go?" bin.

▶ Present your child with the "Where Does it Go?" bin, and explain to her that you want her to help these toys find their homes.

▶ One at a time, take each object from the bin and ask your child to help the lost toy or material find its way back home.

▶ This activity is a great way to introduce new toys and materials and a wonderful opportunity to practice picking up!

▶ Try selecting items such as socks, backpacks, and dirty clothes that often have a hard time finding their way to their respective "homes!"

*You can download this activity and the other at-home activities in this book at www.centerforresilientchildren.org/SSES.

132　　SOCIALLY STRONG, EMOTIONALLY SECURE

The Be-By-Myself Box

Invites children to join you in creating a be-by-myself space for the classroom.

What Children Will Learn

Children benefit from knowing there is a safe place to retreat to when they are overwhelmed or need a break from the larger group. Just like adults, children need their own space to help them relax and regroup from time to time. When we help them create this type of space in their learning and play environments, we show them that we understand how important "alone time" can be to feeling recharged and ready to rejoin play with friends again.

Social and Emotional Skills Supported

Attachment, Initiative, and Self-Control

Materials Needed

contact paper

crayons, markers

empty appliance box (most
    appliance stores will be
    happy to donate boxes)

fabric scraps

paint

photos of the children and
    their families

pillows and other soft items

What to Do

▶ Talk with the children about how at certain times during the day they may want to "get away from it all" and be by themselves.

▶ Show them the places in your classroom where they currently can go to be by themselves.

▶ Next, introduce the large cardboard box, explaining that this will become a new be-by-myself place.

▶ Together with the children, decide where the box will end up once it is finished.

▶ Next, work with the children to determine the rules for how to use their new be-by-myself space. (Remember the guidelines on creating rules shared on page 21.)

▶ Write up these rules (add pictures if possible), and post them in or near the box.

▶ Now, you are ready to work on creating this space!

▶ Taking the box, cut one side completely open as this will serve as the entrance to the be-by-myself area.

▶ Working in small groups and spreading the tasks out over several days you can:

    ◀ Paint the exterior of the box with the children. Invite them to join you in choosing the colors and designs you paint on the box. Allow the box to dry.

    ◀ Add photos from families and those collected from the classroom to the inside of the box. The children's drawings can be added as well.

    ◀ To soften the inside of the box you can purchase foam from your local craft or fabric store and add it to the bottom of the box. Cover the foam with a blanket and add soft pillows and stuffed animals.

▶ Place the box in its space, review the rules regularly, and enjoy!

Social & Emotional Lenses

Do you have a be-by-myself place? Do you respect your loved ones when they need to retreat for a bit and be in their own be-by-myself places? We all need a little peace and quiet sometimes!

The Be-By-Myself Box

Try this activity at home to reinforce the importance of having spaces to be alone!

What Your Child Will Learn
Your child benefits from knowing there is a safe place to retreat to when he is overwhelmed or needs a break from the larger group. Just like you, your child needs his own space to help him relax and regroup. When you help create this type of space you show him that you understand how important "alone time" can be.

Materials Needed

contact paper	fabric scraps
crayons, markers	paint
empty appliance box (most appliance stores will be happy to donate boxes, or, you can always use a table with a long sheet overtop as well!)	photos of your child and family
	pillows and other soft items

What to Do

▶ Talk with your child about how at certain times during the day he may want to "get away from it all" and be by himself.

▶ Show him the places in your home where he can go to have some quiet time.

▶ Next, introduce the large cardboard box, explaining that this will become a new be-by-myself place.

▶ Together with your child, decide where the box will end up once it is finished.

▶ Next, work with your child to determine the rules for how to use the new be-by-myself space.

▶ Write up these rules (add pictures if possible), and post them in or near the box.

▶ Now, you are ready to work on creating this space!

▶ Cut one side completely open as this will serve as the entrance to the be-by-myself area.

▶ Over several days you can:

   ◀ Paint the exterior of the box with your child. Invite him to join you in choosing the colors and designs you paint on the box. Allow to dry.

   ◀ Add photos or drawings to the inside of the box.

   ◀ To soften the inside of the box , purchase foam from your local craft or fabric store and add it to the bottom of the box. Cover the foam with a blanket and add soft pillows and stuffed animals.

▶ Place the box in its space, review the rules regularly, and enjoy!

*You can download this activity and the other at-home activities in this book at www.centerforresilientchildren.org/SSES.

Wall of Fame

Provides storage and display areas to keep projects before and after they have been completed.

What Children Will Learn

When children see their creations displayed, they learn to take pride in what they do, take care of their own things, and respect the work of others.

Social and Emotional Skills Supported

Attachment and Initiative

Materials Needed

art supplies for decorating (glitter, buttons, crayons, markers, yarn, and so on)

clothespins (one per child)

nails

stars cut from card stock or construction paper (one per child)

string that will be hung across one wall in your room

tape or hot glue gun

What to Do

▸ Find space in the classroom where you can hang children's individual work (on the walls, hanging from the ceiling with string and clips, backs of shelving units, doors, and so on).

▸ Explain to the children that each of them will have a star of their own. The star will be for keeping art projects safe while they are working on them and then displaying them when they are finished.

▸ Give the children art supplies and encourage them to decorate their stars any way they wish.

▸ After their stars have dried, secure a clothespin on the back with either tape or a hot glue gun (adult step only). The clothespin attached to the back of the star will allow for easy display (and removal) of projects.

▸ Hang the string from two nails along an empty wall or across the length of your classroom. Stars can also be placed directly onto an empty wall.

▸ Hang the stars along the string by clipping the clothespin to the string. Try to place stars approximately 9-12 inches apart to allow for art to hang without overlap. Call it the "Wall of Fame," and begin adding the children's work!

▸ When the children share their work with you, ask open-ended questions such as:

"How did you decide what to (draw, paint, write, and so on)?"

"What made you choose these (colors, materials, words)?"

"How does this creation make you feel?"

"If you had to give this a title, what would you call it and why?"

▸ Let the children decide when they want to add new creations to their stars.

Social & Emotional Lenses
When you take your time to work on a project, how good do you feel when someone really appreciates it and eagerly puts it on display? Children feel the same; let them know you value their work!

Try hanging your child's creations in this way so that your child knows how much you appreciate her hard work.

What Your Child Will Learn

When your child sees her creations displayed, she learns to take pride in what she does, take care of her own things, and respect the work of others.

Materials Needed

art supplies for decorating (glitter, buttons, crayons, markers, yarn, and so on)

clothespins

nails

star cut from card stock or construction paper

string that will be hung across one wall in your home

tape or hot glue gun

What to Do

▶ Find space in your home where you can hang your child's work (on the walls, hanging from the ceiling with string and clips, backs of shelving units, doors, and so on).

▶ Give your child the star and art supplies, and help her decorate it however she'd like.

▶ Once her star has dried, place a clothespin on the back with either tape or a hot glue gun (adult step only).

▶ Hang the string from two nails along an empty wall (or the place of your choice), add the caption "Wall of Fame," and begin adding your child's work with the clothespins!

▶ Whenever your child shares her work with you, ask open-ended questions like:

"How did you decide what to (draw, paint, write, and so on)?"

"What made you choose these (colors, materials, words, and so on)?"

"How does this creation make you feel?"

"If you had to give this a title, what would you call it and why?"

▶ Your child will bring home so many special creations over the course of her early school years and it may not be possible to save each one. Consider taking your child's picture with her creations as a memento to reflect on together as your child gets older.

My Family Place Mats

Creates a friendly and welcoming atmosphere for all who enter.

What Children Will Learn

Children love to see pictures and drawings of themselves and those people, pets, places, and things they love the most. Having children create a place mat they can look at and talk about helps children feel more comfortable and confident in handling new settings and/or activities and opens the lines of communication about the most important aspects of their lives.

Social and Emotional Skills Supported

Attachment and Initiative

Materials Needed

clear contact paper

colored construction paper cut into place mat size

crayons, markers, paint, and other materials for decorating

glue

pictures of the children and their family members, pets, and special things and/or places

What to Do

▶ Talk with the children about what a place mat is and what it is used for, and that it marks a special place at the table.

▶ Allow the children to pick their two favorite colors of construction paper to be used to create their place mats. Tape each child's pieces of construction paper together.

▶ Give the children their photographs. Encourage their initiative and creativity by allowing them to glue the photographs anywhere they want on the construction paper. Invite them to add other decorative items, as long as the place mat can still lie flat.

▶ After the photos and other decorative items have dried, cover the front and back of the place mats with contact paper or laminate them.

▶ Use the place mats when the children want to work with clay or dough, tabletop projects, and/or eat snacks.

NOTE: Send a note home to parents explaining the activity and asking for pictures of their child and family. Explain that you will return the pictures after you make copies of them. For children whose parents do not send in pictures, have a disposable camera or digital camera available that you can use to take photos of the child in the classroom, as long as the parents have given their permission. If some children prefer to draw all of the pictures, that is great too!

Social & Emotional Lenses
Extend this idea to create place mats with various themes, such as emotions, letters, numbers, seasons, colors, shapes, and more. Simply cut out pictures from magazines or allow children to draw and create their own themed place mats!

Try this activity at home to reinforce your child's feelings of acceptance and inclusion in the family.

What Your Child Will Learn

Your child loves to look at pictures and drawings of himself and those people, pets, places, and things he loves the most. Help him create a place mat to open the lines of communication about the most important aspects of his life.

Materials Needed

clear contact paper

colored construction paper cut into place mat size

crayons, markers, paint, and other materials for decorating

glue

pictures of your child and family members, pets, and special things and/or places

What to Do

▶ Talk with your child about what a place mat is and what it is used for, and the fact that it marks a special place at the table.

▶ Allow your child to pick his two favorite colors of construction paper to create his place mat. Help your child tape the two pieces of paper together.

▶ Give your child the photographs. Encourage his initiative and creativity by allowing him to glue the photographs anywhere he wants on the construction paper. Allow him to add other decorative items, as long as the place mat can still lie flat.

▶ After the photos and other decorative items have dried, cover the front and back of the place mat with contact paper.

▶ Use the place mat when your child wants to work with clay or dough, tabletop projects, meals, and/or snacks.

*You can download this activity and the other at-home activities in this book at
www.centerforresilientchildren.org/SSES.

140　　　　SOCIALLY STRONG, EMOTIONALLY SECURE

Cups of Fun

Provides a range of open-ended materials, from simple to complex, that offers different levels of challenge.

What Children Will Learn

When children take simple objects and manipulate them in ways that are new and exciting to them, it expands their imagination and learning. Open-ended opportunities are created and play possibilities are endless!

Social and Emotional Skill Supported

Initiative

Materials Needed

paper or cardboard cups of varying shapes, sizes, colors, and/or thickness

What to Do

▶ Spend several weeks collecting all sizes and shapes of non-breakable drinking cups.

▶ To generate the children's interest in the cups, lay them all out on a table. Tell the children you would like them to make a tower out of the cups. Challenge them to see how high they can build the tower before it falls. Let them experiment with putting different-sized cups on the bottom, in the middle, and on the top. Talk about what works best and why.

▶ Next, explain that you would like them to come up with new ideas for using these cups. Invite them to share their ideas.

▶ Explain to the children how and where the cups will be stored, and that they are available any time they think of a new idea for using them. Encourage them to share their ideas with you and the rest of the class. Get ready to watch their imaginations soar, and have your camera handy! To expand on the play with this activity, invite children to use the individual theme kits created on page 127 of this resource. Stand back and let the fun begin!

▶ What other everyday materials can you use in new ways? Try pots and pans, measuring spoons and cups, pillows of various shapes and sizes, and so on.

Social & Emotional Lenses
Taking an everyday object and making it into a learning tool challenges children and adults alike to use their creativity!

Cups of Fun

Try this activity at home to reinforce what your child learned about using his imagination!

What Your Child Will Learn

When your child takes simple objects and manipulates them in ways that are new and exciting to him, it expands his imagination and learning. Open-ended opportunities are created and play possibilities are endless!

Materials Needed

cups of varying shapes, sizes, colors, and/or thickness

What to Do

▶ Spend several weeks collecting all sizes and shapes of non-breakable drinking cups.

▶ To generate your child's interest in the cups, lay them all out on a table. Tell your child you would like him to make a tower out of the cups. Challenge him to see how high he can build the tower before it falls. Let him experiment with putting different-sized cups on the bottom, in the middle, and on the top. Talk about what works best and why.

▶ Next, ask your child to come up with new ideas for using these cups. Talk with him about his ideas.

▶ Have the cups readily available for your child, and encourage him to share his ideas with you. Get ready to watch his imagination soar, and have your camera handy!

▶ What other everyday materials can you use in new ways? Try pots and pans, measuring spoons and cups, pillows of various shapes and sizes, and so on.

All About My Feelings

Provides items that help children learn to explore and express their feelings and develop a sense of self.

What Children Will Learn

Children's self-concept comes from defining who they are and what makes them similar to and different from other people. Through their own printing and pictures, "All About My Feelings" books give children the opportunity to create a special book that makes a great addition to any classroom or home library. Children learn that they are unique, and that their friends are interesting and special, too!

Social and Emotional Skills Supported

Attachment, Initiative, Self-Control

Materials Needed

crayons
heavy construction paper or card stock for book cover
hole punch
markers
paper
pencils

What to Do

▶ Start a discussion with the children about feelings. Share with the children that we all have feelings and special ways of showing them.

▶ Let the children know that ALL feelings are acceptable! It is okay to be happy or sad, excited or disappointed. Having a range of feelings is healthy.

▶ Finally, let the children know that what is most important is HOW to express our feelings safely so that we don't hurt ourselves or others.

▶ Explain that together you will make an "All About My Feelings" book to help talk about and understand feelings better.

▶ In this activity you will introduce the children to several "feeling words." Outlined below are the words you will introduce along with a brief definition of the word. You can feel free to use the definition provided or one you think the children may understand better.

◀ Afraid—feeling scared, like something bad might happen

◀ Angry—feeling upset or really mad

◀ Excited—feeling really happy like you want to jump up and shout with joy

- ◄ Happy—feeling great joy and pleasure
- ◄ Lonely—feeling all alone or missing someone you love
- ◄ Loved—feeling like someone really cares about you
- ◄ Proud—feeling good about yourself or something you have done
- ▶ Using the cardstock paper you have available, work with the children to make a book cover entitled "All About My Feelings." Be sure to add the child's name as the author.
- ▶ Ask the children to help you complete each sentence below. Illustrate the page with words and pictures drawn by the children.

  I get scared when...
  I am really happy when...
  I get angry when...
  I get excited when...
  I sometimes become lonely when...
  I feel loved when...
  I am proud of myself when...

- ▶ Start with one page at a time, using the text above as the heading for each individual page. (**NOTE:** This activity can be done over several days or weeks.)
- ▶ When all the pages are complete you can put them together to make a book.
- ▶ To put pages together, use your hole punch to make three holes along the left margin. Then use ribbon to tie the pages together.

Social & Emotional Lenses
Invite children to an "Authors Circle" where they can share their "All About My Feelings" book with the class.

All About Me

Try this activity at home to reinforce your child's view of himself and his peers.

What Children Will Learn

Your child's self-concept comes from defining who he is and what makes him similar to and different from other people. Through his very own print and pictures, your child's "All About Me" book gives him the opportunity to create a picture journal book that makes a great addition to any home library. He will learn that he is special!

Materials Needed

crayons

heavy construction paper or card stock for book cover

hole punch

markers and family photos

paper

pencils

yarn

What to Do

▶ Talk with your child about how wonderful he is. Avoid general statements like, "You are so special" and instead use specific comments about his abilities, accomplishments, interests, and unique characteristics. "Danny, your drawings are so full of details and colors, I think you are a budding artist!"

▶ Explain that you would like your child to illustrate a book about himself. He can also add words and photos if he'd like.

▶ Begin by completing the cover page. Next, move to the other pages within the book.

▶ Your child can complete the pages over a certain period of time, or he can complete it in one sitting. Talk with your child about the pictures and words he adds to his pages while he works on his book.

▶ When the book is ready, use a hole punch and ribbon to tie the pages together.

▶ Invite him to lead an "Author's Circle" where he can read his book to peers, friends, and family.

*You can download this activity and the other at-home activities in this book at
www.centerforresilientchildren.org/SSES.

Let's Get Physical

Helps children release energy throughout the day by providing materials, equipment, and space for indoor gross-motor play.

What Children Will Learn

Moving quickly and slowly with a variety of materials and props helps children develop self-regulatory skills. As children become more aware of their need to release energy and they continue to learn appropriate ways to do so, they become more self-aware. These important skills of self-regulation and self-awareness are key social and emotional skills children will need to succeed in school, and in life!

Social and Emotional Skills Supported

Initiative and Self-Control

Materials Needed

beanbags
box
Nerf® (soft) balls
scarves

What to Do

Activities with No Props:

▶ Simon Says, Red Light/Green Light, Teacher May I?, Partner Shadowing, and just singing and dancing to a variety of types of music are easy activities to implement with few or no props.

Activities with Scarves

▶ Play music of varying tempos, and ask the children to dance to the beat using their scarves.
▶ Invite the children to try to juggle using the scarves.

Activities with Nerf Balls

▶ Encourage the children to play catch with each other.
▶ The children can aim the balls at an indoor hoop, box, bucket, or other appropriate container.
▶ Have pairs or small groups of children sit in a circle and roll the ball back and forth to each other.
▶ Have the children stand in one or more lines and play "over under" with a soft ball, passing it over one child's head and then underneath the next child's legs.

- ▶ Have the children stand with soft balls under their chins, between their knees, between their elbows, or in another position, and then ask them to perform various activities like jumping, dancing, walking backwards, crawling, and so on.
- ▶ Be prepared for giggles throughout the classroom!

Activities with Beanbags
- ▶ Find a box to use as a target.
- ▶ Turn the box upside down, and create several different openings for the beanbag to go through.
- ▶ For each of the openings, have a picture representing an action and words that explain what the child should do—for instance, "Do 10 Jumping Jacks," "Do 10 Toe-Touches," and so on.
- ▶ When they get the beanbag through one of the openings that calls for an action, encourage everyone to do that action together.

Social & Emotional Lenses
Rainy days and days when we can't play outside for other reasons should not be an excuse for children not to release energy! Be creative, and you will find that your day goes more smoothly when you allow children the time they need to exercise!

Try these activities at home to give your child an opportunity to release energy and to practice self-awareness skills.

What Your Child Will Learn

Moving quickly and slowly with a variety of materials and props helps children develop self-regulatory skills. As your child becomes more aware of his need to release energy and he continues to learn appropriate ways to do so, he also becomes more self-aware. These important skills of self-regulation and self-awareness are key social and emotional skills he will need to succeed in school, and in life!

Materials Needed

beanbags

box

Nerf® (soft) balls

scarves

What to Do

Activities with No Props:

► Simon Says, Red Light/Green Light, Mother May I?, Partner Shadowing, and just singing and dancing to a variety of types of music are easy activities to implement with few or no props.

With Scarves:

► Play music of varying tempos, and ask your child to dance to the beat using the scarves.

► Encourage your child to try to juggle the scarves.

With Nerf Balls:

► Roll the ball back and forth to each other.

► Toss the ball back and forth to work on eye-hand coordination.

With Beanbags:

► Find a box to use as a target.

► Turn the box upside down, and create several different openings for the beanbag to go through.

► For each of the openings, have a picture representing an action the child should do; for instance, "Do 10 Jumping Jacks," "Do 10 toe-touches," and so on.

► Have your child throw the beanbag and try to get it through an opening. When he gets a beanbag to go through the opening, encourage him to do what the instructions say.

*You can download this activity and the other at-home activities in this book at
www.centerforresilientchildren.org/SSES.

Free the Toys!

Suggests offering duplicates of favorite items and rotating toys in and out of the play area to keep materials fresh and interesting.

What Children Will Learn

When learning environments become stagnant, children become bored. To keep things interesting, adults need to present new activities, new ideas, and often, toys and materials that were temporarily held captive in storage! Children learn to appreciate old and new items alike, and find exciting ways to engage with materials that, when freed from storage, may seem fresh and new again.

Social and Emotional Skills Supported

Initiative and Self-Control

Materials Needed

empty clear bins for storage and/or full bins of toys that are presently in storage

What to Do

▶ Invite the children to look around the playroom or learning environment and decide which materials the children haven't played with for the past few weeks or months.

▶ Store these materials in clear bins.

▶ Once a week, bi-weekly, or whenever you feel is appropriate (rainy days are great times, too!), bring two or three of the bins out from storage.

▶ Let the children vote on which bin will be "freed" first, second, and third.

▶ Watch in amazement as previously overlooked toys become the central focus for the children!

▶ Do this often to maintain interest in all of your important learning materials.

Social & Emotional Lenses
A change of scenery and new materials are always fun and refreshing for children *and* adults.

Free the Toys!

Try doing this to provide your child with a new and interesting perspective on old toys.

What Your Child Will Learn

When learning environments become stagnant, children become bored. To keep things interesting, adults need to present new activities, new ideas, and often, toys and materials that were temporarily held captive in storage! Children learn to appreciate old and new items alike, and find exciting ways to engage with materials that, when freed from storage, may seem fresh and new again.

Materials Needed

empty clear bins for storage and/or full bins of toys that are presently in storage

What to Do

▸ With your child, look around the playroom and ask which toys he hasn't played with in a while.

▸ Put these toys or sets of materials in clear bins.

▸ Once a week, bi-weekly, or whenever you feel is appropriate (rainy days are great times, too!), bring two or three of the bins out of storage.

▸ Watch in amazement as previously overlooked toys become the central focus for your child!

▸ Do this often to maintain your child's interest in all of his toys.

*You can download this activity and the other at-home activities in this book at
www.centerforresilientchildren.org/SSES.

150   SOCIALLY STRONG, EMOTIONALLY SECURE

References

Barrera, I., Corso, R. M., & Macpherson, D. (2003). *Skilled dialogue: Strategies for responding to cultural diversity in early childhood*. Baltimore, Md: P.H. Brookes Pub.

Bohn, C. M., Roehrig, A. D. & Pressley, M. (2004). The first days of school in the classrooms of two more effective and four less effective primary-grades teachers. *The Elementary School Journal*, 104, 269-287.

Bronfenbrenner, U. (1986). Ecology of the family as a context for human development: Research perspectives. *Developmental Psychology*, 22(6), 723-742.

Brooks-Gunn, J., Berlin, L. J. & Fuligni, Sidle, A. (2000). Early childhood intervention programs: What about the family? Shonkoff, Jack P [Ed], Meisels, Samuel J [Ed]. *Handbook of early childhood intervention* (2nd ed.). New York, NY, US: Cambridge University Press, US; pp. 549-588.

Burchinal, M. R, Peisner-Feinberg, E., Bryant, D. M. & Clifford, R. (2000). Children's social and cognitive development and child-care quality: Testing for differential associations related to poverty, gender, or ethnicity. *Applied Developmental Science*, 4(3), 149-165.

Epstein, A. S. (2009). *Me, you, us: Social-emotional learning in preschool*. Ypsilanti, Mich: HighScope Press.

Espinosa, L. M. (2010). *Getting it RIGHT for young children from diverse backgrounds: Applying research to improve practice*. Upper Saddle River, N.J: Pearson.

Fleer, M., Ed. (1996). *Play Through Profiles: Profiles Through Play*. Watson, Australia: Australian Early Childhood Association Inc.

Gartrell, D. (2004). *The power of guidance: Teaching social-emotional skills in early childhood classrooms*. Clifton Park, NY: Thomson/Delmar Learning.

Greenberg, P. (1992). Ideas That Work with Young Children. How to Institute Some Simple Democratic Practices Pertaining to Respect, Rights, Responsibilities, and Roots in Any Classroom (without Losing Your Leadership Position). *Young Children*, 47(5), 10-17.

Hyson, M. (2003). *The emotional development of young children: Building an emotion-centered curriculum* (2nd ed.). New York: Teachers College Press.

Hyson, M. (2008). *Enthusiastic and engaged learners: Approaches to learning in the early childhood classroom*. New York: Teachers College Press.

Kaiser, B., & Rasminsky, J. S. (2007). *Challenging behavior in young children: Understanding, preventing, and responding effectively* (2nd ed.). Boston, MA: Pearson Allyn and Bacon.

Mashburn, A. J. (2008). Quality of Social and Physical Environments in Preschools and Children's Development of Academic, Language, and Literacy Skills. *Applied Developmental Science*, 12(3), 113-127.

American Academy of Pediatrics., National Resource Center for Health and Safety in Child Care (U.S.), American Public Health Association., & United States. (2002). *Caring for our children: National health and safety performance standards : guidelines for out-of-home child care*. Elk Grove Village, IL: American Academy of Pediatrics.

National Scientific Council on the Developing Child., & Heller School for Social Policy and Management. (2004). *Young children develop in an environment of relationships: Working Paper No. 1.* Waltham, MA: National Scientific Council on the Developing Child, a project of the Heller School for Social Policy and Management at Brandeis University. Retrieved from www.developingchild.harvard.edu

Pianta, R., La Paro, K., Payne, C., Cox, M., & Bradley, R. (2002). The relation of kindergarten classroom environment to teacher, family, and school characteristics and child outcomes. *The Elementary School Journal*, 102(3), 225-238.

Rimm-Kaufman S.E., La Paro K.M., Downer J.T., & Pianta R.C. (2005). The contribution of classroom setting and quality of instruction to children's behavior in kindergarten classrooms. *The Elementary School Journal*, 105(4), 377-394.

Ratcliff, N.J. (2001). Using authentic assessment to document the emerging literacy skills of young children. *Childhood Education*, 78(2), 66-69.

Rodd, J. (1996). *Understanding young children's behavior: A guide for early childhood professionals.* New York: Teachers College Press.

Websites

http://www.devereuxearlychildhood.org
http://www.vanderbilt.edu/csefel/
http://www.cfchildren.org/programs/ssp/overview/

Recommended Resources

Bailey, R. A. (2000). *Easy to love, difficult to discipline: The seven basic skills for turning conflict into cooperation.* New York: William Morrow.

Bredekamp, S. & Copple, C., (2009). *Developmentally appropriate practice in early childhood programs.* (3rd ed.). Washington, D.C: National Association for the Education of Young Children.

Dowling, M. (2000). *Young children's personal, social, and emotional development.* London: P. Chapman Pub.

Epstein, A. S. (2009). *Me, you, us: Social-emotional learning in preschool.* Ypsilanti, Mich: HighScope Press.

FLIP IT. "Four Steps to Building Supportive Relationships that Encourage Emotional Awareness and Emotional Control in Children", e-learning available at https://www.netsmartuniversity.com/flipit/signin.asp.

Gartrell, D. (2004). *The power of guidance: Teaching social-emotional skills in early childhood classrooms.* Clifton Park, NY: Thomson/Delmar Learning.

Hyson, M. (2003). *The emotional development of young children: Building an emotion-centered curriculum* (2nd ed.). New York: Teachers College Press.

Hyson, M. (2008). *Enthusiastic and engaged learners: Approaches to learning in the early childhood classroom.* New York: Teachers College Press.

Katz, L. G., & McClellan, D. E. (1997). *Fostering children's social competence: The teacher's role.* Washington, D.C: National Association for the Education of Young Children.

Kisor, D. (2006). *Songs of Resilience.* North Carolina: Kaplan Early Learning Company.

Koplow, L. (2007). *Unsmiling faces: How preschools can heal.* (2nd ed.). New York: Teachers College Press.

Koralek, D. (1999). *Classroom Strategies to Promote Children's Social and Emotional Development.* Lewisville, NC: Kaplan Early Learning Company.

Koralek, D. (1999). *For Now and Forever: A Guide for Families on Promoting Social and Emotional Development.* Lewisville, NC: Kaplan Early Learning Company.

LeBuffe, P. A., Naglieri, J. A., Koralek, D. G. (1999). *Devereux Early Childhood Assessment Program: Technical Manual.* Lewisville, NC: Kaplan Press.

Masten, A. (2001). *Ordinary magic: Resilience processes in development. American Psychologist,* 56(3), 227-238.

Riley, D. A., San, J. R. R., Klinkner, J., Ramminger, A., Carns, M., Burns, K., Roach, M. A., & Clark-Ericksen, C. (2008). *Social & emotional development: Connecting science and practice in early childhood settings.* St. Paul: Redleaf Press.

Werner, E. E., & Smith, R. S. (1989). *Vulnerable, but invincible: A longitudinal study of resilient children and youth.* New York: Adams, Bannister, Cox.

Werner, E. E. (1990). Protective factors and individual resilience. In S. J. Meisels and J. P. Shonkoff (Eds.), *Handbook of Early Childhood Intervention.* New York: Cambridge University Press, pp. 97-116.

Index